MW00389683

Coastal Cuisine

Coastal Cuisine

Seaside Recipes from Maine to Maryland

Connie Correia Fisher with Joanne Correia

Small Potatoes Press

Copyright © 1999 by Connie Correia Fisher

Edited by Joanne Correia

All rights reserved. No part of this book may be reproduced in any form or by electronic or mechanical means, including information storage and retrieval systems, without permission in writing from the publisher, except by a reviewer who may quote brief passages in review.

Published by Small Potatoes Press
1106 Stokes Avenue, Collingswood, NJ 08108.

Although the author, editor, and publisher have made every effort to ensure the accuracy and completeness of information contained in this book, we assume no responsibility for errors, inaccuracies, omissions, or any inconsistency herein.

ISBN 0-9661200-2-7
Library of Congress Catalog Card Number 99-90464

ATTENTION ORGANIZATIONS, SCHOOLS, AND EDUCATIONAL FACILITIES:
Quantity discounts are available on bulk purchases of this book for educational purposes or fund-raising. Special books or book excerpts can also be created to fit specific needs.

For information, please contact Small Potatoes Press, 1106 Stokes Avenue, Collingswood, NJ 08108. Call (609) 869-5207 or fax (609) 869-5247.

To My Dad

for showing me the beauty in every season

and

To Matthew

who is just beginning to learn

*"Summer cooking implies a sense of immediacy,
a capacity to capture the essence of the fleeting moment."*

— Elizabeth David

CONTENTS

What is the flavor of summer?

I love summer. It is a three month period where "real life" fades away ever so slightly. Suddenly my greatest concerns are proper sunscreen application and yard sales. Weekdays are lighter, and weekends revolve around sand and water.

A bag is quickly packed and I'm in the car, glad for the opportunity to just take off and explore. And there's so much to find . . . funky farmers' markets, unfamiliar beaches, quaint coastal towns, exceptional cafes and restaurants. Sunday nights I sleep happy, warmed from the sun and the wonderful freedom and flavors that summer brings.

Every year I revisit favorite "shore" towns and try to discover new ways to celebrate summer, and I am never disappointed. But then comes September.

All of a sudden "real life returns." The lazy days are over, and everything is rush, rush, rush. Wasn't it just last week I was picking little wild strawberries in Maine, cracking crabs pulled right from the bay in Maryland, licking an ice cream cone on the board-walk in Ocean City, eating lobster rolls on the way home from the Cape, buying Jersey tomatoes from a farmers' market . . . ?

Summer's over and what momento did I bring home to remember my summer holiday? Usually nothing but some sand in my sneakers. All too quickly, the memories of towns and sailboats and beaches fade away. Oh, how I wish the flavor could remain. So I asked the chefs at my favorite seaside haunts if they could help me preserve the taste of summer, packaged up so I could take a little piece of it home. The result is *Coastal Cuisine*, a compilation of over 100 recipes from 65 seaside restaurants, hotels, and inns.

In the winter we hope you use *Coastal Cuisine* to recreate the tastes of summer. Although some recipes call for seasonal ingredients, most can be made all year long, thus extending the summer . . . . at least in your kitchen. And when the weather gets warmer, *Coastal Cuisine* will become a travel guide of good taste. Refer to it often and visit the chefs who so generously donated their favorite recipes.

Like each coastal town, each chef in *Coastal Cuisine* is an artist interpreting the ingredients of summer in his or her own creative way. With that in mind, we have endeavored to keep each recipe in the chef's own voice. You'll notice that procedures vary from recipe to recipe and are not boiler plated as in other cookbooks.

I hope that as you make these dishes, they bring you back to a sunny, warm spot in your mind. After all, the memory of a great meal is the ultimate souvenir.

Best regards,
Connie Correia Fisher
Cherry Hill, New Jersey
(just an hour from the beach!)

"Steep thyself in a bowl of summertime."

— Virgil

Starters and Salads

Crab Pâté

Chef Philip Larson
The Mooring Restaurant, Newport, RI

1 lb. cream cheese
8 oz. canned artichoke hearts, diced
4 oz. snow crab
4 oz. rock crab
2 T. sherry
2 T. lemon juice
1 T. minced fresh parsley
1 T. Outterbridges sherry pepper sauce
$\frac{3}{4}$ tsp. Spanish paprika
1 cup Ritz cracker crumbs

Pulse all ingredients in food processor until smooth. Add crackers and pulse until smooth. That's it! Serve with crackers or crusty bread.

Serves 12 to 15

"Part of the secret of success in life is to eat what you like and let the food fight it out inside."

— Mark Twain

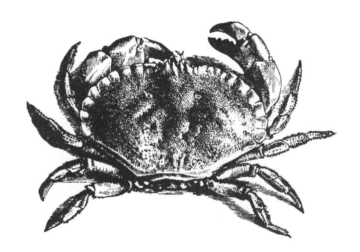

Mushroom Pâté

Innkeeper Joan Wells
The Queen Victoria, Cape May, NJ

1 small onion, finely chopped
2 T. butter
$\frac{1}{2}$ lb. fresh mushrooms, finely chopped
$1\frac{1}{2}$ T. lemon juice
1 tsp. Worcestershire sauce
$\frac{1}{2}$ tsp. salt
dash pepper
2 T. mayonnaise

Sauté onions in butter until soft. Add mushrooms and stir. Add lemon juice, Worcestershire sauce, salt, and pepper. Cook, stirring, until liquids evaporate, about 10 to 15 minutes. Be sure mixture does not brown. Cool; then add mayonnaise to moisten. Chill well. Serve with crackers.

Yields 1 cup

Hommus

Owner Robin Schall
Green Cuisine Restaurant, Stone Harbor, NJ

4 cloves garlic
$\frac{1}{2}$ cup tahini
juice of 2 small lemons or 1 large lemon
4 cups canned garbanzo beans, drained, juice reserved
$\frac{1}{3}$ cup juice from garbanzo beans
$\frac{1}{4}$ tsp. salt

Chop garlic in food processor bowl using knife blade. Add tahini and lemon juice. While food processor is running, gradually add beans, bean juice, and salt. Blend until smooth. Serve with pita bread.

Yields 1 quart

About The Queen Victoria

Most Known For:
hearty, generous buffet breakfast

Years in Business:
20

Most Popular Table:
the big table in the dining room of each building

Chef: Joan Wells

Education/Training:
MA, Museum Studies and US History, University of Delaware

Influences:
years of traveling to country inns and B&Bs

Hobbies:
antique collecting

Favorite Foods:
mashed potatoes from the Ebbitt Room or Waters Edge

Favorite Cookbook:
The Washington Inn's new cookbook

Tuna and Smoked Salmon Timbale

Executive Chef Richard Hyman
Gurney's Inn, Montauk, NY

About Gurney's Inn

Most Known For:
seafood/spa

Years In Business:
50

Most Popular Table:
#10

Chef:
Richard Hyman

Education/Training:
through the ranks in
L.A.

Influences:
fresh ingredients,
seasonality

Hobbies:
photography,
baseball

Hometown:
Brooklyn, NY

Favorite Foods:
Asian, French

Favorite Cookbook:
Gotham Cookbook
by Alfred Portale, *Art
Culinare*, Joel
Robuchon's work

3 large red bell peppers
1 lb. smoked salmon
1 lb. freshest center cut tuna fillet
1 oz. dark sesame oil
1 oz. tamari soy sauce
6 oz. green tobiko caviar (available in most Asian markets)
6 oz. sour cream
olive oil spray

Roast peppers over open flame until skins are blackened. Transfer peppers to a container with a tight fitting lid and allow to cool completely. Remove skins carefully. Cut peppers into a 1/4" dice and set aside.

Slice salmon into 1/4" slices; then dice. Repeat process with tuna, keeping fish separated. Transfer tuna to a small mixing bowl and carefully mix in sesame oil and soy sauce. Keep fishes in refrigerator until ready to assemble.

In a small bowl, carefully stir caviar into sour cream; mix until well incorporated. Reserve about 1 tablespoon.

Lightly spray 6 timbale molds with olive oil. Separate peppers, salmon, tuna, and sour cream mix into 6 equal parts. Fill molds first with tuna, then sour cream, peppers, and finally salmon. Return molds to refrigerator and chill at least 1 hour.

To unmold, invert molds and tap lightly. Serve on a bed of delicate lettuces. Garnish each with a little bit of reserved sour cream mixture.

Serves 6

Polenta Shortcake with Raisins, Figs, and Pinenuts

Executive Chef Rita Tyler
The Woodbox Inn, Nantucket, MA

1 cup cornmeal
pinch salt
$1\frac{1}{2}$ T. olive oil
1 egg
3 T. butter
$\frac{1}{2}$ cup sugar
$\frac{1}{3}$ cup toasted pine nuts
$\frac{1}{3}$ cup golden raisins
1 cup chopped dried figs
2 T. fennel seeds
1 cup all-purpose flour
$\frac{1}{4}$ cup fine bread crumbs

Chef Note

This recipe can also be served as a dessert when topped with ice cream or whipped cream.

Preheat oven to 400°. Bring 2 cups of water to a boil in a medium saucepan. Lower heat to medium and pour in cornmeal in a thin stream. Stir constantly with a wooden spoon. Add salt and olive oil. Stir for 15 seconds or until mixture starts to pull away from the sides of pan. Remove pan from heat.

Add egg, 2 tablespoons butter, sugar, pine nuts, raisins, figs, and fennel seeds; stir until well combined. Add flour and mix well. Smear a 9x13" pan with remaining butter and dust with bread crumbs. Add batter and level with a spatula. Bake for 45 minutes. Cut into squares and serve hot or at room temperature.

Serves 8

Seafood Coquille

Director of Culinary Services Ralph J. Coughenour
Acorns Restaurant at the New England Conference Center
Durham, NH

About Acorns Restaurant

Most Known For:
New England Clam Chowder; voted "Best Brunch on the Seacoast"

Years in Business:
30

Most Popular Table:
"Bird's Nest"

Chef:
Ralph J. Coughenour, CEC, AAC, CFBE

EducationTraining:
ACFEI Certified Executive Chef, member American Academy of Chefs

Influences:
regional and classical cuisine

Hobbies:
collecting CDs and cookbooks

Hometown:
Smithfield, PA

Favorite Foods:
fresh seafood, steaks, chops, pizzas, subs

Favorite Cookbook:
ACF Culinary Olympic Cookbooks 1976-1996

$1\frac{1}{3}$ T. butter
$\frac{1}{2}$ lb. medium shrimp, peeled and deveined
$\frac{1}{2}$ lb. fresh sea scallops
$\frac{1}{2}$ lb. scrod fillets
3 T. dry

Melt butter in sauté pan. Add shrimp, scallops, and scrod. Sauté until just done and remove from pan. Add wine to pan. Simmer until volume is reduced by half. Remove from heat.

Fold cooked seafood, cooking liquid, and crabmeat into seafood sauce. Season with salt and pepper. Refrigerate.

Preheat oven to 400°. Divide mixture into 6 individual casserole dishes. Combine remaining ingredients. Top casserole dishes with cracker mixture. Bake for 20 minutes or until sauce bubbles and crumbs are golden brown.

Serves 6

Crab Mapatello with Roasted Red Pepper Beurre Blanc

Innkeeper/Owner Mark Kulkowitz
The Mad Batter Restaurant at The Carroll Villa Hotel
Cape May, NJ

1 lb. lump crabmeat, shells removed
$\frac{1}{2}$ small onion, diced
1 lb. frozen spinach, thawed, drained, and chopped
$\frac{3}{4}$ lb. ricotta cheese
2 tsp. salt
$\frac{1}{2}$ tsp. white pepper
1 (10x15") sheet puff pastry
Roasted Red Pepper Beurre Blanc (see recipe)

Preheat oven to 350°. Mix crabmeat with onion, spinach, cheese, salt, and pepper.

Soften puff pastry sheet. Cut into 4 squares and trim 1/2" strip from each square to form a "tie." Place equal amounts of crab mixture in the middle of each pastry square. Pull corners up so pastry forms a pouch around crab mix. "Tie" each pouch with pastry strip. Bake for 20 minutes or until golden brown. Serve topped with roasted red pepper beurre blanc.

Serves 4

Roasted Red Pepper Beurre Blanc

1 cup white wine
$\frac{1}{2}$ cup white vinegar
1 T. cracked black
    peppercorns
1 shallot
$\frac{1}{4}$ cup heavy cream
$\frac{1}{2}$ lb. butter
$\frac{1}{2}$ roasted red
    pepper, chopped
salt to taste

Heat wine, vinegar, peppercorns, and shallots in saucepan over medium heat. Reduce to almost dry. Add heavy cream. Allow mixture to reduce and thicken. Slowly whip in butter over low heat, stirring until butter is combined and melted. Strain. Add chopped roasted peppers and salt.

17

Lobster Cocktail

Executive Chef/Owner Adolfo de Martino
Green Gables Restaurant and Inn, Beach Haven, NJ

About Green Gables

Most Known For:
being a restaurant without a menu. The menu changes daily depending on what is fresh and available.

Years In Business:
10

Most Popular Table:
Table 13 located in the corner

Chef:
Adolfo de Martino

Education/Training:
European born and raised

Hobbies:
stone sculpture, clay sculpture, oil and watercolor painting, playing cello

Favorite Foods:
fresh mozzarella (just made, still warm) and semolina bread

Favorite Cookbook:
Marco Pierre White

2 T. balsamic vinegar
6 (1 lb.) lobsters
6 small bunches mache (also known as lamb's lettuce)
4 celery stalks
24 orange segments
1 very ripe papaya, peeled and seeded
2 T. lemon juice
$\frac{1}{2}$ tsp. salt
$\frac{1}{4}$ tsp. white pepper
10 T. extra virgin cold pressed olive oil
6 sprigs lemon thyme

In a large pot of salted, boiling water, add vinegar and lobsters. Simmer for 6 minutes. Drain and rinse under cold water. Set aside. When cool enough to handle, crack shell and remove the tail and claw meat. Slice each tail — on the bias — into 6 pieces.

Gently clean mache with a damp paper towel. Arrange mache in 6 oversized martini glasses. Shave each celery stalk to expose the tender core. Make 24 shavings from the 4 stalks — 4 shavings per glass. Alternate the celery shavings and orange segments around the glasses. Mound lobster chunks in the center of the glasses. Dice papaya into 1/2" cubes, about 24 to 30 pieces. Place papaya on top of mache and lobster.

Whisk together lemon juice, salt, and white pepper. Add the olive oil in a stream. Combine thoroughly and drizzle a bit over each lobster cocktail. Finish with a sprig of lemon thyme.

Serves 6

Angels on Horseback

Executive Chef Michael Cajigao
Phillips by the Sea, Ocean City, MD

2 oz. olive oil
$\frac{1}{2}$ small onion, diced
1 (12 oz.) bag spinach, destemmed and chopped
2 oz. licorice liqueur such as anisette or sambuca
12 strips bacon, lightly cooked (2 to 4 minutes)
48 oysters, shucked and removed from shell, shells reserved
8 oz. grated provolone or mozzarella cheese

Heat oil in large skillet over medium heat. Sauté onion until translucent. Add spinach and liqueur. Stir continuously 1 to 2 minutes. Remove from heat and refrigerate 20 minutes.

   Preheat oven to 400°. Slice bacon strips into quarters. Wrap 1 piece around each raw oyster. Evenly divide the spinach and place on top of each oyster shell. Place wrapped oyster on spinach bed. Top each with grated cheese. Bake for 6 to 8 minutes or until cheese is melted and light brown.

Serves 8

About Phillips by the Sea

Most Known For:
Maryland-style crab dishes and fresh fish

Years in Business:
30

Most Popular Table:
Oceanfront

Chef: Michael Cajigao

Education/Training:
2-year apprenticeship while earning a B.S. in Hotel Management

Influences:
infusing regional styles with local ingredients

Hobbies:
cycling, travel, going to restaurants

Hometown:
Randolph, NJ

Favorite Foods:
any seafood

Favorite Cookbook:
anything by Paul Prudhomme

Salmon Cakes

Chef Philip Larson
The Mooring Restaurant, Newport, RI

$1\frac{1}{4}$ lb. salmon, poached in 1 quart bouillon, cooled, and flaked
$\frac{3}{4}$ cup mayonnaise
1 cup Italian bread crumbs
2 large eggs
2 T. diced Bermuda onion
1 T. diced red bell pepper
$\frac{1}{2}$ T. minced fresh parsley
$\frac{1}{4}$ tsp. dill
$\frac{1}{4}$ tsp. Coleman's dry mustard
dash salt, pepper, Tabasco, and Worchestershire sauce
melted butter

Preheat oven to 400°. Combine all ingredients except butter. Mix by hand and form into 8 cakes. Dust cakes with additional bread crumbs. Splash top with melted butter. Bake approximately 15 to 20 minutes or until brown.

Serves 8

Martin House Salt Cod Cakes with Tomato Basil Jam

Chef Alex Mazzocca
Martin House Restaurant, Provincetown, MA

$\frac{1}{2}$ lb. soaked salt cod, fresh or frozen
$\frac{1}{2}$ cup mashed potatoes
1 T. lemon zest
1 T. lemon juice
$\frac{1}{2}$ small red onion, minced
$\frac{1}{4}$ large carrot, minced
$\frac{1}{4}$ red bell pepper, minced
1 T. chopped fresh basil
1 tsp. capers
1 egg, beaten
1 T. Dijon mustard
$\frac{1}{4}$ cup bread crumbs
olive oil
Tomato Basil Jam (Recipe appears on page 111.)

Soak salt cod for 2 to 3 hours or overnight. Cook salt cod in boiling water for 20 minutes. Drain well. In a food processor, mix salt cod, potatoes, zest, and lemon juice. Add vegetables, basil, and capers; mix well. Add egg and mustard; mix again. Add enough bread crumbs so that mixture is soft enough to form cakes but still quite moist.

Form 8 cakes approximately 2" across and 2" high. Roll cakes in extra bread crumbs. Heat olive oil in sauté pan and brown cakes on both sides. Transfer to 400° preheated oven to finish (about 7 to 8 minutes).

Serve with Tomato Basil Jam.

Serves 8 as appetizer
4 as entree

About Martin House Restaurant

Most Known For:
atmosphere,
creative fine dining

Years in Business:
9

Most Popular Table:
"T3"

Chef:
Alex Mazzocca

Education/Training:
courses at the
Culinary Institute of
America and N.Y.
Restaurant School

Influences:
the seasons,
international travel

Hobbies:
travel, gardening

Favorite Foods:
Mediterranean and
Asian

Favorite Cookbook:
Vongerichten's book

Atlantic County Ostrich with Jersey Tomato and Corn Relish

Owner Larry Boylan
The Inn at Sugar Hill, Mays Landing, NJ

12 oz. ostrich fan (or other tender cut), cut into 1/2 to 3/4"
  thick steaks
salt and pepper
olive oil
2 oz. brandy or white wine
4 cups mesclun or other young greens
Jersey Tomato and Corn Relish (Recipe appears on page 109.)

Season steaks on both sides with salt and pepper. Heat olive oil in large sauté pan until very hot. Sauté steaks 2 to 3 minutes on each side or until rare/medium rare. Deglaze pan with liquor; reduce until just a glaze is left on meat.

  Place 1 cup of greens on each plate and top with 1/4 of relish. Slice the steaks into 1/2" slices and place around the plate.

Serves 4

ChefNote

The ostrich I use is from a local farm in Atlantic County. Since all ostrich meat has one third the fat of beef and half the fat of chicken, you must try not to cook it past medium-rare or it will start to become tough. If cooked properly, ostrich can be as tender as filet mignon. Enjoy!!!

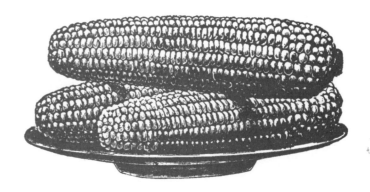

Pear and Almond Salad

Assistant Executive Chef Roger Morgan
Bally's Park Place, Atlantic City, NJ

2 Bosc pears, julienned
1 cup mixed gourmet greens
4 shiitake mushrooms, stems removed and julienned
1 T. julienned fresh ginger
$\frac{1}{2}$ cup toasted almond slices
Sherry Vinaigrette (see recipe)

Combine first 5 ingredients. Fold into sherry vinaigrette.
Toss salad. Serve chilled or at room temperature.

Serves 4

Sherry Vinaigrette

$\frac{1}{2}$ T. chopped shallots
1 tsp. chopped garlic
$\frac{1}{4}$ cup sherry wine
 vinegar
1 cup olive oil
1 T. sugar
$\frac{1}{2}$ T. chopped parsley
$\frac{1}{2}$ T. chopped chives
$\frac{1}{2}$ tsp. cayenne
 pepper

Whisk all ingredients together.

Cranberry Salad with Walnuts and Gorgonzola

Executive Chef Cynthia Sikes
Galaxy Bar & Grille, Ocean City, MD

1 head romaine lettuce, torn into large pieces
$\frac{1}{4}$ cup whole walnuts
$\frac{1}{4}$ cup fresh whole cranberries
$\frac{1}{4}$ cup crumbled Gorgonzola cheese
2 T. julienned red onion
3 oz. Cranberry Dressing (see recipe)

Combine salad ingredients in a large bowl; then toss with
cranberry dressing. Serve immediately.

Cranberry Dressing

1 cup cranberry juice
$\frac{1}{2}$ cup rice wine
 vinegar
1 cup walnut oil
$\frac{1}{4}$ cup light corn syrup
$\frac{1}{2}$ cup cranberries
$\frac{1}{2}$ cup whole walnuts
salt and pepper

Puree ingredients
in a blender until
smooth. Season
with salt and
pepper to taste.

Yields 1 quart

Soups and Stews

Maine Lobster Bisque

Executive Chef Fredric Link
Rose Garden Restaurant in Bar Harbor Hotel-Bluenose Inn
Bar Harbor, ME

2 (1½ lb.) live Maine lobsters
2 T. flour
4 T. unsalted butter, softened
3 T. olive oil
3 T. diced shallots
1 tsp. minced garlic
3 T. diced celery
2 T. diced carrots
4 oz. brandy
2 oz. white wine
3 cups fish stock or water
1 T. tomato paste
1 tsp. chopped fresh thyme
1 tsp. chopped fresh tarragon
2 tsp. chopped fresh parsley
1 bay leaf
cracked black peppercorns to taste
2 oz. heavy cream
salt to taste

"Only the pure of heart can make a good soup."

— Ludwig van Beethoven

In a large pot, bring 4 quarts water to a rapid boil. Place lobsters in pot and cover. Boil for 8 to 10 minutes. When finished cooking, remove lobsters and place in large bowl with iced water to chill down. Once chilled, remove lobsters from water and break tails, claws, and knuckles from body of lobster. Set lobster bodies aside. Crack tails and remove tail meat (keeping meat intact). Slice tail meat in half, vertically; set aside. Crack claws and knuckles and remove meat (keeping meat intact); set aside.

In small bowl, mix flour and butter together into a small ball. With large knife or meat tenderizer, smash lobster bodies and claw, tail, and knuckle shells into small pieces. In saucepan, heat olive oil over medium heat. Add smashed lobster pieces and sauté for 3 minutes. Add shallots, garlic, celery, and carrots. Sauté for 10 seconds.

Remove pan from heat and add brandy. Return pan to heat. Add white wine, stock or water, tomato paste, thyme, tarragon, 1 teaspoon parsley, bay leaf, and cracked peppercorns. Simmer 12 to 15 minutes.

Remove pan from heat and crumble butter and flour mixture into pan until it blends with broth. Return pan to heat and simmer on low for 5 minutes. Add heavy cream and stir 2 to 3 minutes.

Using a fine strainer, strain liquid into another saucepan while pushing down on shells to squeeze out all the liquid. Place this saucepan over low heat. Add salt to taste. Bring bisque to a simmer. Add tail meat; cook for 30 seconds. Add claw and knuckle meat; cook an additional 45 seconds.

Place half of tail, 1 claw, and knuckle meat each into each of 4 bowls. Pour bisque over lobster meat and garnish with remaining parsley. Serve with French bread.

Serves 4

About Rose Garden Restaurant

Most Known For:
AAA Five Diamond rating; American regional cuisine with French technique

Years in Business:
5

Chef:
Fredric Link

Education/Training:
degree from Kendall Culinary College in Evanston, IL; apprenticed at Ritz-Carlton Hotel in Chicago

Influences:
working at the Ritz-Carlton Dining Room with Chef Sarah Stegner and all the chefs there; fresh products that are available during the summertime in New England

Hometown:
Chicago, IL.

Favorite Foods:
all fresh seafood

Lobster Bisque

Owner Jim Filip
Doris & Ed's, Highlands, NJ

$1\frac{1}{2}$ sticks ($\frac{3}{4}$ cup) unsalted butter
3 (11.3 oz.) cans frozen lobster meat, thawed with liquid
    reserved
$\frac{3}{4}$ cup all-purpose flour
$1\frac{1}{2}$ tsp. fine sea salt
$\frac{1}{2}$ tsp. cayenne or to taste
2 qts. half-and-half
$\frac{1}{4}$ cup medium-dry sherry such as Sandeman's Amontillado

Coarsely chop lobster meat. In a heavy kettle melt butter
over low heat. Stir in lobster meat and reserved liquid.
Cover and cook over low heat, stirring occasionally, for 25
minutes. Stir in flour, salt, and cayenne. Cook over low heat,
stirring constantly, for 10 minutes.

    In a large saucepan, heat half-and-half just until it
"smiles" (barely simmers; do not boil). Add half-and-half and
sherry to lobster mixture and cook, stirring, at a bare
simmer for 10 minutes. Do not boil.

    Bisque may be made 2 days ahead. Cook completely
and then store covered in refrigerator. Reheat bisque over
low heat, stirring until hot.

Yields 16 cups

Chef Tip

This recipe calls for frozen lobster meat. Do not substitute fresh, as the liquid produced when thawing frozen canned lobster is essential to the bisque.

Quahog "Chowdah"

Chef/Owner David Twining
Nantuckets, Fenwick Isle, DE

$\frac{1}{2}$ lb. butter

1 cup scallops

3 cups white corn

1 cup diced onion

1 cup diced celery

1 lb. red potatoes, diced

1 tsp. thyme

$\frac{1}{4}$ cup parsley

1 qt. clam juice

3 cups shucked top neck clams

3 oz. Worcestershire sauce

1 cup heavy cream

Melt butter in large pan and lightly sauté scallops, corn, onion, celery, potatoes, thyme, and parsley. Add juice and bring to a boil. Lower heat and simmer 15 minutes. Add clams and Worcestershire sauce and simmer for 5 minutes. Remove from heat and add cream.

Serves 4

About Nantuckets

Most Known For:
seafood

Years in Business:
9

Chef:
David Twining

Education/Training:
23 years

Influences:
fresh seafood

Hobbies:
golf, swimming, eating

Favorite Cookbook:
Vincent Price's book

New Jersey Clam Chowder

Executive Chef Luigi Baretto
Ram's Head Inn, Absecon, NJ

2 pts. half-and-half
1 cup clam juice
1 medium onion, diced
$\frac{1}{2}$ tsp. chopped garlic
2 T. flour
10 oz. cream of asparagus soup (canned or your own recipe)
3 New Jersey tomatoes, cut and seeded
24 New Jersey chowder clams, chopped
1 cup diced, precooked white potatoes
1 tsp. celery powder
$\frac{1}{2}$ tsp. pepper
$\frac{1}{2}$ tsp. paprika
$\frac{1}{2}$ tsp. thyme
1 cup precooked New Jersey asparagus spears

"Worries go
down better with
soup than
without."

— Jewish Proverb

Combine half-and-half with clam juice in a saucepan and bring to a boil. In a soup pot, sauté onion and garlic until golden. Add flour and stir. Add hot half-and-half mixture and whip until smooth. Add the cream of asparagus soup, tomatoes, clams, potatoes, and spices. Mix well. Bring to a boil; reduce heat, and let simmer for 10 to 15 minutes, stirring often. Additional clam base can be added to taste. Garnish with asparagus spears.

Serves 6

Long Island Mussels in Beer Broth

Executive Chef/Partner Donald P. Sullivan
Southampton Publick House, Southampton, NY

1 lb. Shinnecock Bay mussels, debearded and rinsed
8 oz. Southampton India Pale Ale
4 T. butter
3 cloves garlic
1 T. chopped fresh thyme
1 T. chopped fresh parsley
salt and pepper to taste
2 sprigs thyme
sliced lemon

Put mussels, pale ale, 2 tablespoons butter, garlic, thyme, parsley, and salt and pepper into a large saucepan. Heat until mussels are steamed open (about 6 to 8 minutes).

Melt remaining butter for dipping purposes and place in a small serving dish. Serve mussels in large bowl. Garnish with thyme sprigs and lemon. Serve with crusty bread and ice cold Southampton Golden Lager.

Serves 6

Onion Soup

Innkeeper Ruth Keyes
Red Brook Inn, Old Mystic, CT

6 cups sliced Bermuda onions
$\frac{1}{4}$ cup butter
3 T. flour
7 cups beef broth
1 tsp. salt
$\frac{1}{8}$ tsp. pepper
2 T. red wine or cider vinegar

In large iron kettle, sauté onions in 2 tablespoons butter until lightly browned. Add remaining butter and flour and whisk until smooth. Add broth, salt, and pepper and simmer for 1 hour. Add wine or vinegar and serve with homemade soda crackers.

Serves 6

Butternut Squash Bisque

Executive Chef Karl L. Patton C.C.C., C.H.C.
Three Chimneys Inn, Durham, NH

2 lbs. butternut squash, peeled and seeded
5 cups chicken stock
$\frac{1}{2}$ cup brown sugar
nutmeg to taste
cinnamon to taste

Simmer squash in the chicken stock until the squash is very soft. Remove from heat and place into blender. On high speed, whip in the brown sugar, cinnamon, and nutmeg.

Serves 4 to 8

Black Ale Onion Soup

Executive Chef/Partner Donald P. Sullivan
Southampton Publick House, Southampton, NY

2 T. butter
12 Spanish onions, peeled and sliced
$\frac{1}{4}$ cup diced garlic
8 oz. Publick House Porter
1 qt. beef stock
2 tsp. Kitchen Bouquet
2 T. chopped thyme
2 T. chopped parsley
salt and pepper to taste
6 slices baguette bread, toasted
6 ($\frac{1}{4}$") slices mozzarella cheese

Melt butter in large stock pot. Sauté onions and garlic until tender. Add porter; simmer 15 minutes. Add stock and seasonings. Bring to boil, then reduce heat and simmer for 30 minutes.

Pour soup into 6 ovenproof soup crocks. Float 1 slice of bread on top of soup; then top with cheese slice. Broil until cheese melts (about 2 minutes). Serve piping hot.

Serves 6

Sesame-Jalapeño Soup

Owner Melissa Jasper
The Friendly Toast, Portsmouth, NH

1 large onion, chopped
3 T. butter
$1\frac{1}{2}$ cups tahini
$1\frac{1}{2}$ qts. heavy cream
1 cup EITHER lowfat milk or vegetable stock
1 cup minced jalapeños
1 tsp. ground ginger
2 tsp. cayenne
$\frac{1}{2}$ tsp. nutmeg
1 T. salt
1 T. black pepper

In a large saucepan, sauté onions in butter until translucent. Add all other ingredients and heat over medium flame. Garnish with fresh cilantro if desired.

Serves 6 to 8

Mushroom Barley Soup

Chef/Partner David Graham
Van Scoy's Bistro, Cape May, NJ

4 oz. raw pearled barley

2 cups water

1 cup coarsely chopped onion

$1\frac{1}{2}$ T. olive oil

$\frac{3}{4}$ lb. domestic mushrooms, sliced

$\frac{1}{4}$ lb. shiitake caps, sliced into strips

$\frac{1}{4}$ lb. portobella mushroom stems and caps, gilled and sliced
into strips

3 T. naturally fermented soy sauce

2 T. pale dry cocktail sherry

$\frac{1}{2}$ tsp. salt

$\frac{1}{2}$ tsp. ground black pepper

1 T. minced fresh garlic

2 tsp. peeled and minced fresh ginger root

5 cups vegetable stock

Bring barley and water to a boil. Reduce heat; cook until barley is tender. Add more water if needed. Set aside.

In a large pot, sauté onion in olive oil over moderate heat. When onions are translucent, add mushrooms, stirring frequently. As mushrooms shrink, add remaining ingredients except stock and barley. Cook for 5 minutes. Add stock and barley. Bring to a boil; reduce heat and simmer 30 minutes. You may serve immediately, but like most soups, Mushroom Barley is best when heated and served the next day.

Yields 10 cups

About Van Scoy's Bistro

Most Known For:
eclectic international cuisine

Years in Business:
7

Most Popular Table:
at the end of the deck under the tree

Chef: David Graham

EducationTraining:
20 years in food service

Influences:
numerous tropical and sub-tropical dining experiences

Hobbies:
baseball, basketball, music, reading

Hometown:
Baltimore, MD

Favorite Foods:
curries, Ethiopian food, Thai dishes

Favorite Cookbook:
Revised Moosewood

Thai Fruit Soup

Executive Chef Rita Tyler
The Woodbox Inn, Nantucket, MA

About The Woodbox Inn

Most Known For:
bananas Foster, beef Wellington, homemade pop-overs — all the consistent favorites

Years In Business:
generations. The Woodbox, built in 1709, is Nantucket's oldest inn and only James Beard listed restaurant.

Most Popular Table:
in front of the fireplace

Chef:
Rita Tyler

Education/Training:
The Restaurant School in Philadelphia

Hobbies:
growing orchids, wine collecting, reading

Favorite Foods:
Northern Italian

Favorite Cookbook:
Marcella Hazan's

1 cup chopped cantaloupe
1 cup chopped honeydew melon
1 cup chopped ripe mango
1 cup chopped ripe peaches
2 cups mango puree
2 cups orange or pineapple juice
3 T. fresh lime juice
$\frac{1}{2}$ cup sugar
2 T. peeled and finely chopped ginger root
3 pints mango, strawberry, or raspberry sorbet or a
    combination of the three
$\frac{1}{4}$ cup crystallized ginger pieces
fresh mint for garnish

Puree fruits, juices, sugar, and ginger root in batches in a blender or food processor. Chill for at least 3 hours, preferably longer, to allow flavors to blend. Serve in shallow bowls with a scoop of sorbet and garnish with crystallized ginger and fresh mint.

Serves 8

Blueberry-Lemon Soup

Owner/Innkeeper Kim O'Mahoney
The Inn at Portsmouth Harbor, Kittery, ME

1 pt. blueberries (Wild Maine blueberries are preferred.)
1 cup water
$\frac{1}{2}$ cup sugar
1 lemon, thinly sliced
1 cinnamon stick
1 cup plain lowfat yogurt plus extra for garnish
2 T. freshly squeezed lemon juice
2 T. confectioners' sugar
ground cinnamon

Combine berries, water, sugar, lemon, and cinnamon stick in a saucepan. Bring to a boil over medium heat. Reduce heat and simmer 15 minutes. Cool. Remove cinnamon stick. Process in blender until smooth. Chill overnight.

When ready to serve, combine yogurt, lemon juice, and confectioners' sugar. Whisk into blueberry mixture. Garnish with a swirl of yogurt and sprinkle of cinnamon.

Serves 6

About The Inn at Portsmouth Harbor

Most Known For:
breakfasts and dinners that highlight Maine's regional and seasonal specialties

Years in Business:
11

Chef:
Dennis Hayden

Education/Training:
self-taught

Influences:
the abundance of Maine's bounty of seafood

Hobbies:
cooking, raising puppies for Guide Eyes for the Blind

Favorite Foods:
fish of any kind, chocolate cake in a bowl with milk — yum!

Vegetarian Chili No Con Carne

Chef/Owner Mary McCabe
Bridges Restaurant on the Bay, Ocean City, NJ

About Bridges Restaurant on the Bay

Most Known For:
seafood, soups, and vegetarian dishes

Years in Business:
4

Most Popular Table:
by the fireplace

Chefs:
Mary McCabe and Peter Caprio

Education/Training:
Kushi Institute and long time cooking at various restaurants

Influences:
love and making people happy

Hobbies:
photography, reading, hiking

Hometown:
Ocean City, NJ

Favorite Foods:
vegetables, pasta, seafood

Favorite Cookbook:
Japanese, Italian, Spanish, French

4 cloves garlic, chopped
$\frac{1}{2}$ cup EACH chopped green, red, orange, and yellow peppers
$\frac{1}{2}$ cup EACH chopped carrots, celery, and onion
$\frac{1}{4}$ cup chopped tomato
4 cups cooked beans (Great northern, black, red kidney, anasazi, navy, black turtle, and lentils are best. Aduki are not recommended.)
1 cup diced seitan or wheat meat
2 to 4 cups water (vary according to desired wetness of chili)
$\frac{1}{3}$ cup chopped cilantro
$\frac{1}{4}$ cup chopped parsley and/or scallions
1 T. EACH cumin and chili powder
cayenne pepper to taste

In a large pot, sauté garlic and vegetables until soft. Add beans, seitan, and water. Add herbs and spices. Simmer until flavors blend together, about 15 minutes. Serve alone or with Mary's Salsa (Recipe appears on page 110.)

Serves 6 to 8

Lobster and Sweet Potato Stew

Executive Chef Laurence deFreitas
Mews Restaurant, Provincetown, MA

1 (46 oz.) can clam juice (or your own fish stock)
3 ($1\frac{1}{2}$ lb.) live lobsters
9 T. clarified butter
2 cups chopped shallots
1 cup diced celery
zest of 2 lemons
$\frac{1}{2}$ cup chopped fresh tarragon
1 cup dry vermouth
$1\frac{1}{4}$ cups brandy
2 qts. heavy cream
salt and pepper to taste
3 ripe tomatoes, diced
$\frac{1}{4}$ cup dry white wine
Stewed Sweet Potatoes (Recipe appears on page 94.)

In a very large stock pot with a lid, bring clam juice to a boil. Add lobsters, cover, and cook for 5 minutes. Remove lobsters and cool. Remove meat from shell and cut into chunks. Set meat aside.

In a large saucepan, sauté lobster shells in 6 table-spoons butter. Add shallots and celery and cook until vegetables are tender. Add lemon zest and tarragon. Deglaze pan with vermouth and 1 cup brandy. Add heavy cream and heat until liquid is reduced by half. Strain liquid, pressing down to extract all liquid from shells. Season liquid (cream) with salt and pepper and reserve. Discard solids.

In a separate pan, sauté lobster meat in remaining butter over medium high heat. Stir in tomatoes. Increase heat and add remaining brandy, white wine, lobster cream, and stewed sweet potatoes. Gently stir and heat through. Serve in bowls with warm crusty bread.

Serves 6

Chef Note

"Cape Cod lobsters are best, of course," says general manager Ron Robin, "but you can use the ones from Maine!"

Celsius Bouillabaisse Setoise

Executive Chef Jean-Luc Charpentier
Celsius Restaurant and Tapas, Rehoboth Beach, DE

About Celsius Restaurant and Tapas

Most Known For:
bouillabaisse

Years in Business:
3

Most Popular Table:
round booth

Chefs:
M.J. Stanton and
Jean-Luc Charpentier

Education/Training:
 M.J. is self-trained.
Jean-Luc trained in
Paris.

Hobbies:
M.J. reads and does
yoga; Jean-Luc's
into swimming and
bike riding

Favorite Foods:
lamb, seafood

Favorite Cookbook:
favorite authors are
Daniel Boulud and
Yves Thuries

$\frac{1}{4}$ cup olive oil
2 large onions, peeled and chopped
2 large green peppers, seeded and cut into large pieces
2 large red peppers, seeded and cut into large pieces
2 large garlic cloves, peeled and chopped
2 large fennel bulbs, quartered
5 stalks celery, cut into chunks
1 large bay leaf
8 large tomatoes, peeled and chopped
2 cups fish stock, fresh if possible
1 cup white wine
pinch saffron
4 T. chopped parsley
1 lb. EACH salmon, mahi mahi, and sea bass, cut into chunks
36 raw shucked clams or mussels
18 large raw shrimp, cleaned
3 ($1\frac{1}{2}$ lb.) lobsters, raw, cut in half
$\frac{1}{4}$ cup Pernod
salt and pepper

Heat oil in a large stock pot. Sauté onions, peppers, garlic, fennel, celery, and bay leaf for 10 minutes. Add tomatoes, stock, wine, saffron, and parsley. Cover and simmer 15 minutes. Add fish, clams or mussels, and shrimp; cook covered for 10 to 15 minutes. Add lobster meat and Pernod; cook covered for 15 minutes. Season with salt and pepper.

Serve in large bowls. A good hearty bread and a fine white wine with this meal makes for a most delightful evening.

Serves 6

124's Bouillabaisse

Executive Chef Chris LaMotte
124 Cottage Street Restaurant, Bar Harbor, ME

$\frac{1}{3}$ cup olive oil

1 cup diced onions

1 T. minced garlic

2 (8 oz.) cans whole plum tomatoes in juice

1 (8 oz.) can chopped sea clams, juice drained and reserved

1 cup white wine

2 tsp. lobster base

3 bay leaves

$\frac{1}{2}$ T. fennel seeds

$\frac{1}{2}$ tsp. thyme

1 tsp. saffron

dash Tabasco sauce

salt and pepper to taste

$\frac{3}{4}$ to 1 lb. fresh seafood (shrimp, mussels, scallops, lobster, swordfish, tuna, or any combination), cut into medium-sized cubes.

Heat olive oil in a large saucepan. Lightly sauté onion and garlic until translucent. Crush whole tomatoes (preferably by hand) and add to onions. Add clam juice, white wine, lobster base, bay leaves, fennel, thyme, saffron, Tabasco, and salt and pepper. Bring to a boil, then simmer over medium low heat. Add clams and seafood; heat until seafood is cooked through. Finished bouillabaisse should have lots of broth. If your stock reduces too much, just add water. Garlic bread is a nice accompaniment.

Serves 4 to 6

About 124 Cottage Street

Most Known For:
gourmet salad bar

Years in Business:
20

Most Popular Table:
overlooking the garden

Chef:
Chris LaMotte

Education/Training:
apprenticeship

Hobbies:
fishing, hiking

Hometown:
Flemington, NJ

Favorite Foods:
seafood

Favorite Cookbook:
Escoffier's *Le Guide Culinaire*

Meats, Fowl, and Game

Spice Encrusted Seared Pork Tenderloin with Mustard Sauce

Assistant Executive Chef Roger Morgan
Bally's Park Place, Atlantic City, NJ

Mustard Sauce

1 cup cider vinegar
1 cup prepared
  mustard
3 T. ketchup
$\frac{1}{4}$ cup molasses
  <u>or</u> honey
$\frac{1}{4}$ cup water
1 T. Tabasco sauce
1 T. Worcestershire
  sauce
2 T. salted butter

Combine all ingredients except butter and simmer for 4 to 5 minutes. Remove from heat and add butter. Serve over pork, chicken, potatoes, or veggies.

$\frac{1}{2}$ cup olive oil
1 T. whole grain mustard
$\frac{1}{4}$ cup chopped parsley
$\frac{1}{4}$ cup chopped fresh lemon thyme
2 T. cracked black pepper
1 T. toasted ground cumin seed
1 T. toasted ground coriander seed
1 T. kosher salt
2 tsp. ground allspice
2 (1 lb.) tenderloins of pork, silver skin removed
Mustard Sauce (see recipe)
Mashed Sweet Potatoes, optional (Recipe appears on
  page 95 .)
Pear and Almond Salad, optional (Recipe appears on
  page 23.)

Preheat oven to 375°. Combine olive oil and mustard. In a separate bowl, combine herbs and spices. Coat pork tenderloins first with oil and mustard mix; then generously coat with spice mix. Place on cooking pan and roast until internal temperature is 155° or until firm to touch.

Cut roasts into 1/4" slices. Fan slices on serving plate and drizzle with mustard sauce.

If serving the roasts with optional sides, the following presentation is recommended. Place mashed sweet potatoes in the center of 4 plates. Fan out slices of pork tenderloin in front of sweet potatoes. Place pear and almond salad behind sweet potatoes. Drizzle mustard sauce around the outside of the dish.

Serves 4

44

Boneless Pork Chops in Dijon Ale Sauce

Executive Chef/Partner Donald P. Sullivan
Southampton Publick House, Southampton, NY

$\frac{1}{4}$ cup Dijon mustard
1 T. chopped parsley
1 T. chopped shallots
1 T. chopped garlic
4 (4 oz.) pork tenderloin chops
2 T. olive oil
6 oz. Southampton India Pale Ale
6 oz. chicken stock
4 oz. heavy cream
1 T. butter
salt and pepper to taste

Combine mustard, parsley, shallots, and garlic. Rub mixture on both sides of chops. Marinate in refrigerator for up to 3 hours.

Preheat oven to 350°. Heat oil in heavy gauge pan over high heat. Quickly add chops; sear both sides for 2 minutes each. Remove chops from pan and finish in oven for approximately 5 minutes. Add India Pale Ale to pan to deglaze. Add stock and reduce liquid by half. Add cream and butter; reduce by half. Season with salt and pepper. Plate chops and top with sauce.

Serves 2

About Southampton Publick House

Most Known For:
microbrewery/ restaurant

Years in Business:
3

Chef:
Donald Sullivan

Education/Training:
20 years cooking; master's degree Hotel and Restaurant Management

Influences:
my area's indigenous products

Favorite Foods:
oysters, locally grown vegetables

Veal Chops

Chef/Owner Terri Vorelli
Vorelli's Restaurant, Provincetown, MA

4 thick veal chops
Chop Marinade (see recipe)
2 T. butter
3 shallots, finely chopped
2 T. flour
$\frac{1}{2}$ cup dry white wine
$1\frac{1}{2}$ cups veal stock
pinch of sugar
1 T. Dijon mustard
Roast Vegetables (Recipe appears on page 92.)
chopped fresh parsley

Marinate chops in marinade for 4 hours, turning once.

Remove veal chops from marinade. Sear each side and finish cooking to desired doneness in a 375° oven. (Save drippings from the bottom of the pan for sauce.)

Meanwhile, melt butter in medium saucepan. Add shallots and sauté until soft and golden brown. Remove shallots with a slotted spoon and set aside. Stir flour into pan and continue to stir for 3 to 4 minutes. Return shallots to pan; add white wine, veal stock, and pan drippings. Bring to a boil over medium heat, stirring constantly. Reduce heat; add sugar and mustard and simmer for 15 minutes uncovered.

Ladle some sauce onto each plate. Center the veal chop and surround it with roasted vegetables. Sprinkle fresh chopped parsley around vegetables.

Serves 4

Chop Marinade

1 cup light olive oil
4 garlic cloves, minced
2 shallots, minced
$\frac{3}{4}$ cup red wine
1 tsp. fresh rosemary
1 tsp. fresh thyme
1 tsp. salt
cracked black pepper

Combine all ingredients and mix well.

Mediterranean Veal with Fresh Vegetables

Director of Culinary Services Ralph J. Coughenour
Acorns Restaurant at the New England Conference Center
Durham, NH

6 (6 oz.) veal cutlets, trimmed and pounded flat
Veal Marinade (see recipe)
all-purpose flour
2 oz. olive oil
$\frac{1}{2}$ tsp. minced garlic cloves
$\frac{1}{2}$ lb. fresh mushrooms, quartered
$\frac{1}{2}$ cup zucchini, seeded and diced
$\frac{1}{2}$ cup yellow squash, seeded and diced
2 oz. dry white wine
2 EACH red and green peppers, diced
1 can artichoke hearts, halved
1 can pitted black olives, halved
$\frac{1}{4}$ tsp. crushed red pepper
salt to taste

Submerge veal cutlets in marinade. Let stand for 2 hours.

Remove veal and place vegetables in marinade. Let stand for 10 minutes.

Dredge veal in flour. Heat olive oil in large sauté pan over medium heat. Add cutlets; sauté until browned on one side. Turn cutlets and add garlic, mushrooms, zucchini, and squash. Sauté until squash is tender and veal is browned on second side. Remove veal and keep warm.

Deglaze pan with wine. Add peppers, artichoke hearts, and olives. Add crushed red pepper and continue to cook until heated through. Adjust salt and pepper to taste.

To serve, place veal on plate and top with vegetables. Great when served with angel hair pasta, garlic butter, and Parmesan cheese.

Serves 6

Veal Marinade

1 cup olive oil
$\frac{1}{4}$ cup wine vinegar
1 garlic clove
1 tsp. salt
$\frac{1}{2}$ tsp. white pepper
$\frac{1}{2}$ tsp. celery salt
$\frac{1}{4}$ tsp. cayenne pepper
$\frac{1}{4}$ tsp. dry mustard
dash Durkee Red Hot

Combine ingredients in blender and puree until thoroughly chopped and mixed.

47

Athenian Lamb

Chef/Owner Judith Clayton
Gypsy Sweethearts Restaurant, Ogunquit, ME

About Gypsy Sweethearts

Most Known For:
creative multi-ethnic
cuisine

Years in Business:
20

Most Popular Table:
"C2" on the porch

Chef: Judith Clayton

Education/Training:
B.A. Sociology, self-
taught chef

Influences:
new taste combina-
tions from travel
experiences

Hobbies:
gardening, reading,
photography, baking
off season

Favorite Foods:
goat cheese, flan,
artichokes, ceviche
shrimp, gazpacho

Favorite Cookbooks:
*Emeril's New New
Orleans, Coyote's
Pantry, Silver Palate,
Miami Spice, A Taste
of San Francisco*

1 (5 lb.) boned leg of lamb
1 cup fresh mint leaves
2 T. oregano
4 to 5 cloves fresh garlic, slivered
olive oil
juice from 3 fresh lemons
salt and pepper to taste

Make slits in lamb and insert 3/4 cup mint leaves, 1 tablespoon oregano, and garlic at regular intervals. Pour olive oil
and lemon juice over meat. Rub entire meat surface with
remaining mint and oregano and salt and pepper. Cover
and marinate 24 hours, turning meat several times.

Preheat oven to 500°. Using a deep roaster pan, set
rack in pan, place meat on rack, and then pour water into
bottom of roaster. (Water should not touch meat. It's used
to cut down on splattering.) Sear meat for 20 minutes.
Reduce heat to 425° and cook, basting often, for about 2
hours and 20 minutes or until meat thermometer reads
172°.

Serves 6 to 8

West Indian Curry Chicken

Chef /Owner John C. Albright
C'est La Vie Restaurant, Beach Haven Crest, NJ

3 T. oil or butter
6 to 8 boneless chicken breasts, cubed
1 green pepper, chopped
3 large onions, chopped
1 fresh coconut with milk, meat shredded
$\frac{1}{2}$ cup raisins
4 T. chutney
3 T. raspberry puree
5 T. mild curry powder
2 T. tumeric
salt and pepper to taste
1 pint chicken stock
sliced apples, bananas, pineapples, nuts for garnish

Heat oil or butter in heavy sauté pan over medium-high heat. Sear chicken. Set aside.

In a large pan, sauté green pepper and onions. Add coconut meat and milk, raisins, chutney, raspberry puree, herbs, and salt and pepper. Add chicken stock and simmer for at least 30 minutes.

Add chicken about 15 to 20 minutes before serving. Garnish with sliced apples, bananas, pineapple, and nuts.

Serves 6 to 8

About C'est La Vie

Most Known For:
French cuisine

Years in Business:
1

Most Popular Table:
Table 10

Chef:
John C. Albright

Education/Training:
The Restaurant School, Johnson & Wales University

Influences:
a visual image or discovery of fresh produce

Hobbies:
surfing

Hometown:
Haven Beach, NJ

Favorite Foods:
French and Caribbean seafood

Favorite Cookbook:
The New Larousse Gastronomique and *Le Bec-Fin Recipes* by Georges Perrier

Breast of Chicken Bhutuwa

Director of Culinary Services Ralph J. Coughenour
Acorns Restaurant at the New England Conference Center
Durham, NH

$1\frac{1}{2}$ lb. skinned and boned chicken breasts, cut $\frac{1}{2}$" thick
Marinade (see recipe)
4 T. olive oil
1 tsp. fenugreek seed
5 whole cloves
5 garlic cloves, minced
1 T. minced fresh ginger root
3 red chiles, julienned
$\frac{1}{2}$ tsp. dry mustard
1 cup green peas, thawed
1 cup scallions, sliced into 1" pieces
$\frac{1}{4}$ tsp. cinnamon

Coat chicken thoroughly with marinade. Refrigerate for 2 hours.

In large sauté pan, heat olive oil over medium heat. Sauté fenugreek seeds in oil until they turn dark. (Do not burn.) Add cloves and sauté for 30 seconds. Add chicken; sauté until well browned.

Add garlic, ginger, red chiles, and dry mustard. Reduce heat. Continue to cook until chicken in cooked through. (A little water or white wine may be added to deglaze if desired.) Add green peas, scallions, and cinnamon. Stir for 2 to 3 minutes. Drain off any excess oil. Serve with rice pilaf, pita, and stir-fried veggies.

Serves 4

Bhutuwa Marinade

1 T. fresh lemon juice
1 T. olive oil
$\frac{1}{3}$ tsp. dry mustard
1 T. cumin powder
1 T. tumeric
1 tsp. black pepper
dash salt

Combine ingredients and mix well.

50

Bombay Chicken

Executive Chef Chris LaMotte
124 Cottage Street Restaurant, Bar Harbor, ME

2 (6 oz.) boneless chicken breasts
1 cup all-purpose flour
1 large apple, sliced into wedges and soaked in lemon juice
$\frac{1}{2}$ cup raisins
$\frac{1}{2}$ cup fancy coconut
$\frac{1}{2}$ cup salted half cashews
Curry Sauce (see recipe)

Preheat oven to 375°. Dust chicken with flour and lightly brown chicken in a medium sauté pan.

Towel dry apple wedges. Combine apples with raisins, coconut, and cashews. Place chicken in the bottom of a baking dish. Cover each chicken breast with curry sauce. Top with fruit mixture. Bake for 15 to 20 minutes or until chicken is baked through and the topping is lightly browned.

Serves 2

Curry Sauce

1 T. butter
1 T. flour
1 cup half-and-half
2 tsp. curry powder
1 chicken bouillon
   cube
salt and pepper

In a small sauce-pan, melt butter. Stir in flour until well blended. Add remaining ingredients and allow to thicken. Season with salt and pepper to taste.

Grilled Szechuan Breast of Duck

Chef/Owner Neil R. Elsohn
Waters Edge Restaurant, Cape May, NJ

1 whole duck breast, boned and trimmed of excess fat
$\frac{1}{2}$ cup Szechuan Vinaigrette (Recipe appears on page 108.)
1 oz. roasted sesame oil
1 red bell pepper, julienned
1 cup stemmed and sliced shiitake mushrooms
8 oz. cooked lo mein noodles
2 oz. butter, cut into little cubes
$\frac{1}{2}$ cup sliced scallions

Cut duck into 4 equal pieces. Marinate duck in 1/4 cup vinaigrette (or enough to cover) in refrigerator for at least 3 hours or preferably overnight.

Grill duck to medium rare and keep warm.

Add roasted sesame oil to sauté pan and heat until almost smoking. Add peppers and shiitakes and cook until wilted. Add lo mein noodles, remaining vinaigrette, and butter. Toss until heated through. Divide among 4 plates. Slice duck breast and fan on top of noodles. Garnish with scallions.

Serves 4

"One cannot think well, love well, sleep well, if one has not dined well."

— Virginia Wolfe,
A Room of One's Own

Moullard Duck Breast

Executive Chef Chris Hubert
The Ebbitt Room, Cape May, NJ

2 Moullard duck breasts
salt and pepper
3 T. olive oil
1 cup potato gnocchi
1 cup Hubbard squash, blanched and diced
2 T. chopped parsley
1 T. chopped chive
1 tsp. chopped sage
$\frac{1}{4}$ cup Calvados
2 cups duck stock
1 oz. butter
$\frac{1}{4}$ cup pumpkin seeds
Quince Puree (see recipe)
4 sprigs chervil

Preheat oven to 350°. Score duck breast, fat side up, and season well with salt and pepper. In a heavy skillet, heat 1 tablespoon olive oil over medium flame until smoking. Sear duck, fat side down, for 5 minutes. Discard rendered fat. Turn duck breast and place in oven. Cook for 10 to 15 minutes, until medium rare. Remove from oven and allow duck to rest.

In salted water, blanch potato gnocchi until 75% cooked; then shock in cold water.

In a heavy skillet, sauté squash for 2 minutes. Add parsley, chives, and sage. Deglaze with Calvados. Allow liquid to reduce. Add duck sauce. Reduce again. Add gnocchi and season with salt and pepper. Add butter and simmer until blended.

Preheat oven to 300°. Toss pumpkin seeds in remaining olive oil. Season with salt and pepper. Toast in oven for 6 minutes.

To serve, place small piles of squash and gnocchi on 4 plates. Top with sliced duck breast. Top duck with a dollop of quince puree. Drizzle sauce around and garnish with pumpkin seeds and chervil.

Serves 4

Quince Puree

1 T. butter
2 quince, chopped
$\frac{1}{2}$ cup white wine
$\frac{1}{2}$ cup chicken stock
salt and pepper
nutmeg

In a heavy saucepan, heat butter. Add quince and sauté 3 minutes. Add white wine and chicken stock. Cook for 10 minutes. Strain and puree. Season with salt, pepper, and nutmeg.

Roast Marinated Quail

Executive Chef Chris Hubert
The Ebbitt Room, Cape May, NJ

4 semi-boneless quails
salt and pepper to taste
$\frac{1}{4}$ cup plus 2 T. white balsamic vinegar
$\frac{3}{4}$ cup olive oil
1 T. chopped shallot
1 tsp. chopped garlic
1 sprig EACH thyme, rosemary, basil
1 bay leaf
$\frac{1}{4}$ cup red wine
$\frac{1}{8}$ cup blackstrap molasses
1 T. cocoa powder
1 cup veal stock or bouillon
1 T. butter
Pumpkin Relish (Recipe appears on page 109.)

Season quail with salt and pepper. Mix vinegar and oil. Add shallots, garlic, and herbs. Cover quail with marinade and refrigerate 6 hours or overnight.

In heavy saucepan, heat wine over medium flame until liquid is reduced by half. Stir in molasses and cocoa and simmer a few seconds. Add veal stock or bouillon and simmer a few minutes. Whip in butter. Remove from heat and reserve.

Preheat oven to 350°. In heavy skillet, sear marinated quail on both sides until golden brown. Cook quail in oven for 10 minutes. Remove quail from oven. Let rest a few minutes and then quarter.

Place quail on serving platter. Top with relish. Drizzle warm sauce over quail.

Serves 4

Grilled Quail

Executive Chef Kenneth W. Koon
Woody's Restaurant, Rehoboth Beach, DE

4 quails, bones and back removed
2 cups soy sauce
2 T. fresh chopped dill
1" fresh ginger root, grated
2 garlic cloves, pressed
1 head cabbage, shredded
1 head radicchio, shredded

Combine soy sauce, dill, ginger, and garlic. Pour over quails, reserving 1/2 cup. Cover and refrigerate overnight.

Heat grill (hickory chips are suggested). Toss together cabbage and radicchio. Grill quails, turning and brushing with marinade every 90 seconds until done (about 6 minutes). Serve atop cabbage and radicchio. Nap with reserved sauce.

Serves 4

Venison with Game Sauce

Executive Chef Luigi Baretto
Ram's Head Inn, Absecon, NJ

12 (2 oz.) venison rosettes (medallions)
1 cup flour
$\frac{1}{2}$ cup vegetable oil
$1\frac{1}{2}$ oz. brandy liquor
salt and black pepper to taste
1 cup Game Sauce (Recipe appears on page 102.)
4 Potato Leek Planks, optional (Recipe appears on page 92.)

Dust venison with flour. Heat oil and sauté venison quickly, browning evenly on both sides. Remove venison, discard oil, and deglaze pan with brandy and salt and pepper. Add sauce. Return venison to pan and cook until medium rare. To serve, display rosettes over potato leek planks and nap with sauce.

Serves 4

We may live without poetry, music and art;

We may live without conscience, and live without heart;

We may live without friends; we may live without books;

But civilized man cannot live without cooks.

—Owen Meredith,
Lucile

Seafood and Shellfish

Tuna with Honey Mustard Ginger Sauce

Chef/Owner George Pechin
Peaches at Sunset, Cape May, NJ

About Peaches at Sunset

Most Known For:
touches of Thai cuisine

Chef: George Pechin

Education/Training:
Culinary Institute of America, apprentice under several chefs

Influences:
travel

Hobbies:
gardening and travel

Hometown:
Pottstown, PA

Favorite Foods:
ethnic — Thai, Vietnamese, Eastern European, Mexican

Favorite Cookbook:
Cuisine of Hungary and *The Cake Bible*

1 qt. heavy cream
1 2" piece ginger, peeled and julienned
3 T. Dijon mustard
2 T. honey
salt and pepper to taste
4 (8 to 10 oz.) pieces tuna
oil

Combine cream and ginger in a saucepan and bring to a boil; then lower heat so that sauce just simmers. Stir occasionally with a wooden spoon until sauce reduces by at least half. Remove from heat and strain sauce. Add Dijon mustard and honey. Add salt and pepper to taste.

Season tuna with oil and salt and pepper. Cook tuna on a hot grill or in a sauté pan about 3 minutes per side or to desired doneness (should be red or pink inside).

Divide sauce between 4 plates and top with tuna.

Serves 4

Tortilla-crusted Sea Bass with Black Bean Sauce

Owner Larry Boylan
The Inn at Sugar Hill, Mays Landing, NJ

4 (6 to 8 oz.) fillets striped bass
salt and pepper
1 cup ground corn tortilla chips (I use red corn chips.)
vegetable oil
Black Bean Sauce (Recipe appears on page 108.)
Roasted Corn Salsa (Recipe appears on page 110.)

Season fish with salt and pepper. Press flesh side of fillets into tortilla crumbs to coat. Heat oil in heavy sauté pan over medium-high heat. When oil is hot, place fish in pan — crumb side down — and cook until golden. Flip over, lower heat, cover pan, and cook until flesh is firm and flakes with a fork.

Place some of the bean sauce onto the plate. Center the fish on the sauce and top with some of the salsa. Garnish the plate with some extra corn chips.

Serves 4

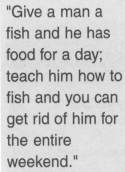

"Give a man a fish and he has food for a day; teach him how to fish and you can get rid of him for the entire weekend."

— Zenna Schaffer

Chilean Sea Bass Gilhop

Executive Chef John H. Pohlig
Henry's on the Beach, Cape May, NJ

8 (7 to 8 oz.) sea bass fillets
Spice Rub (see recipe)
1 lb. unsalted raw butter
juice of 2 lemons, strained
juice of 2 limes, strained
$1\frac{1}{4}$ cups granulated sugar
$\frac{1}{2}$ cup clarified butter
pinch salt

Wash fish in cold water and pat dry. Coat fillets with spice rub.

Cut unsalted butter into 1" cubes and place in small pot. Add lemon and lime juices and sugar. Heat over lowest flame possible, stirring constantly, until butter is just melted and sauce is luke warm. Set aside.

Preheat oven to 350°. In a medium sauté pan, heat clarified butter and salt on medium-high heat. When very hot, add fillets. Cook on one side until almost black; turn fillets over and repeat. Finish cooking fillets in oven for 8 to 10 minutes.

To serve, pour some sauce onto each plate and top with a fillet and additional sauce.

Serves 8

Spice Rub

1 cup cajun spice mix
$\frac{1}{2}$ cup paprika
$\frac{1}{3}$ cup all-purpose flour
$\frac{1}{3}$ cup granulated sugar

Combine all ingredients. Store in an airtight container.

Pepper Encrusted Nantucket Swordfish

Owner/Manager John C. Zartarian
The Paddock Restaurant, Hyannis, MA

4 (8 oz.) pieces fresh swordfish, 1" thick
4 oz. five peppercorn mix, crushed coarsley
4 T. canola oil
4 T. whole butter
4 T. chopped shallots
8 oz. cognac or brandy
8 oz. heavy cream
8 oz. lightly thickened stock (chicken or veal)
salt and pepper to taste

In a large nonstick skillet, heat oil over medium-high flame until hot. Press crushed peppercorns on one side of fish. Sear on peppercorn side for 3 minutes; turn over and cook other side for another 3 minutes. Remove fish from pan and set aside.

    Drain oil from pan. Add butter and shallots to hot pan and cook for 2 minutes. Remove pan from fire and add brandy to deglaze pan. Return pan to fire and allow alcohol to burn off. Add stock, heavy cream, and fish and finish cooking until sauce thickens. Serve immediately. Add salt and pepper to taste and enjoy!

Serves 4

About The Paddock Restaurant

Most Known For:
local fresh seafood, the freshest produce artfully prepared

Years in Business:
30

Chef:
John Anderson

Education/Training:
Culinary Institute of America

Influences:
Food Arts, Food and Wine, Gourmet

Hobbies:
wood carving, gardening

Hometown:
Norwich, MA

Favorite Foods:
Italian

Favorite Cookbook:
anything by Emerill Lagasse

Grilled Salmon with Mango and Lime Vinaigrette

Executive Chef Richard Cole
Coonamessett Inn, Falmouth, MA

About Coonamessett Inn

Most Known For:
contemporary American and New England dining

Years in Business:
since the early '50s

Chef: Richard Cove

EducationTraining:
Culinary Institute of America

Influences:
Food Network; trendy, hot chefs

Hobbies:
golf

Hometown:
Red Hook, NY

Favorite Foods:
anything Asian and spicy

Favorite Cookbook:
New Tastes from Texas, Paul Bocuse's French Cooking, and *Emeril's New New Orleans Cooking*

$\frac{1}{4}$ cup mango puree
juice of 1 lime
1 tsp. chopped ginger
1 T. sliced scallions
1 tsp. chopped cilantro
2 T. soy sauce
1 T. sesame oil
1 tsp. chopped garlic
2 T. canola oil
1 T. rice wine vinegar
1 tsp. Sirachi (red chili paste available in Asian markets)
16 spears standard size asparagus
olive oil
2 (8 oz.) salmon fillets

Combine first 11 ingredients and blend with a hand blender. Set aside.

Coat asparagus with olive oil and grill until grill marks appear. Grill salmon approximately 4 minutes on each side.

To serve, place 8 asparagus spears on each plate, top with salmon, and nap with vinaigrette.

Serves 2

Pesto-crusted Salmon with Roasted Tomato Oil

Owner Larry Boylan
The Inn at Sugar Hill, Mays Landing, NJ

1 cup fresh basil leaves
2 to 3 cloves garlic
2 T. Parmesan cheese
3 T. roasted pecans
extra virgin olive oil
plain bread crumbs
4 (6 to 8 oz.) salmon fillets
salt and pepper to taste
Roasted Tomato Oil (see recipe)

In food processor, blend basil, garlic, Parmesan cheese, and pecans to form a dry paste. Add enough olive oil to produce a runny paste. Scrape into bowl and add bread crumbs until crust has a slightly moist crumb texture. Set aside.

Preheat oven to 375°. Season salmon with salt and pepper. Apply a thin (about 1/8") coat of crust to meat side of each fillet. Place salmon in baking dish — pesto side up — and drizzle with olive oil. Bake until desired doneness, about 8 to 10 minutes per inch of thickness of fish. Place fillets on plates. Drizzle with tomato oil.

Serves 4

Roasted Tomato Oil

3 ripe plum tomatoes, halved and seeded
salt and pepper
2 cloves garlic
1 cup extra virgin olive oil

Roast tomatoes in a 400° oven until dry and starting to char. Let cool a bit. Place in blender with remaining ingredients and puree.

Strawberry Barbecued Salmon

Executive Chef Jim Koch
The Tun Tavern Brewery & Restaurant, Atlantic City, NJ

About The Tun Tavern

Most Known For:
beer!

Years in Business:
1

Chef:
Jim Koch

Education/Training:
Academy of Culinary Arts, Mays Landing, NJ

Influences:
culinary TV shows, magazines, other chefs

Hobbies:
eating out

Hometown:
Brigantine, NJ

Favorite Foods:
garlic steamers and crabs with lots of beer

Favorite Cookbook:
The Inn at Little Washington

1 cup honey
1 cup hot sauce (I like Durkee Red Hot.)
juice of 1 orange
2 oz. Jack Daniel's Tennessee whiskey
4 (10 oz.) salmon fillets
1 pint fresh strawberries, sliced

In a small bowl whisk together the honey, hot sauce, orange juice, and Jack Daniel's.

Preheat oven to 350°. On a hot grill, cook salmon fillets until medium rare and grill marks appear. Top each with 3 ounces sliced strawberries and coat with hot sauce mixture. Finish cooking in oven until desired doneness. (I recommend you serve with sautéed spinach and garlic and mashed potatoes.)

Serves 4

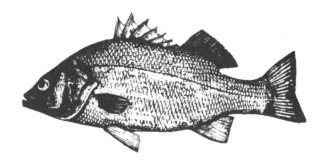

Sweet Potato-crusted Salmon

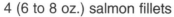

Executive Chef Kenneth W. Koon
Woody's Restaurant, Rehoboth Beach, DE

4 (6 to 8 oz.) salmon fillets
1 large sweet potato, peeled and sliced paper thin
2 cup flour
4 oz. clarified butter
8 sun-dried tomatoes, cut in half and reconstituted
4 tsp. capers
$\frac{1}{2}$ cup Madeira wine
kosher salt and fresh ground pepper to taste

Cover front and back of salmon fillets with potato slices. Cover and refrigerate for 1 hour.

Preheat oven to 400°. Heat large ovenproof skillet until a single drop of water dances on it before evaporating. Dust crusted fillets with flour. Add butter to pan; then fillets. Turn when golden brown. After 1 minute, add tomatoes, capers, and wine. Season with salt and pepper. Put pan in oven and cook fillets to desired doneness (about 4 minutes). Serve topped with tomato, caper, and wine sauce.

Serves 4

"[Advise] the ruler to govern the state as one cooks a small fish — that is, don't turn it so often in the pan that it disintegrates."

— Lao Tzu

Whole Red Snapper with Sweet and Sour Sauce

Executive Chef Cynthia Sikes
Galaxy Bar & Grille, Ocean City, MD

2 whole red snappers, cleaned, scaled, and scored
$\frac{1}{4}$ cup flour
oil for frying
1 cup julienned leeks
Ginger Sweet and Sour Sauce (see recipe)

Coat fish lightly with flour; shake off excess. Preheat hot fryer to 375°. Place fish in fryer so that head is touching tail. Fry until fish is done through to center. Remove from fryer and set on paper towel to drain. Add leeks to hot oil; fry until lightly brown. Place on paper towel to drain.

Line bottom of serving bowl with fried leeks and top with fish. Pour hot ginger sauce over entire fish.

Serves 2

Ginger Sweet and Sour Sauce

1 T. peanut oil
1 T. minced garlic
1 T minced shallots
1 T. minced ginger
$\frac{1}{4}$ cup white wine
$\frac{1}{4}$ cup rice wine vinegar
$\frac{1}{4}$ cup soy sauce
1 (12 oz.) bottle ketchup
$\frac{1}{4}$ cup brown sugar

In a small saucepan, heat oil over medium high heat. Add garlic, shallots, and ginger; sauté 1 minute. Add white wine and vinegar; cook 1 minute. Add remaining ingredients. Heat through and strain.

Roasted Halibut and Brill with Corn Crab Confit

Chef/Owner Fredric Byarm
Fredric's Restaurant, West Creek, NJ

1 medium onion, diced
2 large carrots, diced
1 celery stalk, diced
1 lb. fish bones
3 bay leaves
1 tsp. whole cloves
1 T. whole black peppercorns
2 cups dry white wine
4 oz. lemon juice
4 (7 oz.) halibut fillets
salt and freshly cracked black pepper
olive oil
Mashed Potatoes (Recipe appears on page 95.)
Corn Crab Confit (Recipe appears on page 98.)
4 sprigs rosemary or purple basil

Heat oven to 400°. Place onion, carrots, celery, fish bones, bay leaves, cloves, and black peppercorns into roasting pan and cook 30 minutes or until vegetables are dark brown in color. Remove from oven and place all ingredients in small stock pot over high heat. Add 1 cup wine and enough water to cover bones. Bring to a boil; reduce heat and simmer 20 minutes. Strain and discard all solids. Cook remaining broth over medium heat until only 1/4 of volume remains. Add remaining wine, lemon juice, and 2 cups water. Reduce again by half. Set aside.

Season fillets with salt and pepper. Heat olive oil in sauté pan. When smoking hot, add fillets, flesh side down; sear until medium brown. Turn fillets over. Place pan in preheated 375° oven; bake 12 to 15 minutes to finish cooking.

To serve, divide mashed potatoes between 4 plates. Top with confit; then fillet. Pour heated brill around plate. Garnish with fresh sprig of rosemary or purple basil.

Serves 4

About Fredric's Restaurant

Most Known For:
eclectic American

Most Popular Table:
fireside

Chef:
Fredic Byarm

Education/Training:
Restaurant School of Philadelphia

Hobbies: running, skiing, jazz

Hometown:
Stafford Township, NJ

Favorite Foods:
salmon

Favorite Cookbooks:
Great Women Chefs by Julie Stillman

Beech Tree Inn Baked Fish Pimento

Innkeeper Kathy Wudyka
The Beech Tree Inn, Newport, RI

1 (10.5 oz.) can tomato soup
$\frac{1}{3}$ cup Sauterne, Chablis, or other white dinner wine
1 cup shredded mild Cheddar cheese
$\frac{1}{2}$ small jar pimentos, chopped
1 small onion, minced
2 T. chopped parsley
4 fish steaks (halibut, salmon, sole or cod)

Combine soup, wine, cheese, and pimentos in saucepan. Stir over low heat until cheese melts and is well blended. Add onion and parsley.

Preheat oven to 375°. Arrange fish steaks in shallow baking dish and cover with sauce. Bake 25 minutes or until fish flakes with a fork.

Serves 4

Bluefish Paupiettes with Thyme and Basil

Executive Chef/Owner Adolfo de Martino
Green Gables Restaurant and Inn, Beach Haven, NJ

6 lbs. bluefish, boned and skinned (see Chef Note)
3 T. olive oil plus oil for preparing foil squares
2 large onions, finely diced
$\frac{1}{3}$ cup brandy
6 sprigs fresh thyme
1 tsp. salt
$\frac{1}{2}$ tsp. black pepper
4 T. fresh bread crumbs
12 (7x7") squares aluminum foil
6 mozzarella slices, halved
12 basil leaves, washed and dried
2 T. butter
2 T. oil

In a large nonstick skillet, heat oil over medium-high flame until hot (but not smoking). Add onions; sauté until translucent.

Add diced bluefish and cook, turning once or twice, until just opaque. Pour in the brandy. (Be careful, it will flame up.) Let alcohol burn off. Remove pan from heat. Crumble the thyme into the mixture and add salt, pepper and bread crumbs. Toss several times to mix. Let cool.

Using a pastry brush, coat 1 side of the foil squares with oil. On each square, using a meat mallet, flatten a large bluefish piece (a 4 to 6 ounce portion) to cover about 2/3 of the foil.

Preheat oven to 400°. Reserve about 1 cup of the onion/bluefish mixture. Divide the remaining mixture among the 12 flattened portions to cover half of each piece of bluefish. Top slice of mozzarella and 1 basil leaf. Roll into a cigar or tube, squeezing both ends like a candy wrapper. Wrap foil around roll. Bake on cookie sheet for 15 minutes. Cool and remove foil. Heat butter and oil in a skillet. Brown bluefish in skillet. Top with reserved onion/blue fish mixture.

Serves 6

Chef Note

To prepare bluefish fillets for cooking, all dark flesh should be removed from the thickest part of the fillet. With a super sharp knife, split large fillets in half to facilitate the removal of the dark flesh. With the blade slanted (almost parallel to fillet) and following the grain of the flesh, cut out and discard all the dark meat. Cut the fillets into 12 (4 to 6 ounce) portions plus 30 to 40 small diced pieces.

Mediterranean Style Rainbow Trout

Chef John Amodie
La Bec Rouge, Hampton, NH

$\frac{1}{4}$ cup olive oil
2 (8 oz.) trout fillets, butterflied
$\frac{1}{2}$ red onion, diced
1 T. chopped fresh garlic
1 T. fresh basil, chiffonade
$\frac{1}{2}$ cup red wine
2 T. chopped fresh spinach
2 ripe plum tomatoes, diced
1 T. sliced black olives
8 oz. crushed tomatoes
pinch cayenne pepper
$\frac{1}{2}$ lb. cooked tricolored pasta shells

In a sauté pan, warm olive oil over high heat. Sauté trout (skin side up) for 2 minutes or to desired doneness. Remove fish from pan and keep warm.

Add onion, garlic, and basil to the same pan. Sauté until onion is lightly browned. Add wine, spinach, tomatoes, and black olives. Lower heat and simmer for 3 minutes. Add crushed tomatoes and cayenne pepper and heat until warmed through.

To serve, divide pasta between 2 plates. Top with sauce and trout. If desired, garnish with additional black olives and tomato.

Serves 2

Grilled Rainbow Trout in Grape Leaves

Executive Chef Karl L. Patton C.C.C., C.H.C.
Three Chimneys Inn, Durham, NH

4 tsp. whipped unsalted butter
4 tsp. crushed and minced capers
salt and pepper to taste
4 (5 oz.) rainbow trout fillets, pinbones removed
8 sprigs fresh dill
4 freshly steamed grape leaves
2 medium yellow tomatoes
3 T. olive oil
1 tsp. garlic
$\frac{1}{2}$ ripe papaya, peeled and seeded

Bring butter to room temperature; then with a fork mix in the capers and salt and pepper. Apply evenly but not liberally to the top of each trout fillet. Add 2 sprigs of dill to the top of each fillet. Wrap each fillet tightly with 1 grape leave. Refrigerate for approximately 30 minutes.

Pan-roast tomatoes in olive oil until lightly browned; then remove skin and seeds. Briefly sauté garlic. Puree tomatoes, garlic, and papaya together in a blender and refrigerate.

On a preheated grill, cook fillets approximately 4 minutes on each side or until fish is tender and flaky. Serve fillets flattened with grape leaves butterflied open and napped with the sauce.

Serves 4

"Give me books, fruit, French wine and fine weather, and a little music played by someone I do not know."

— John Keats

Macadamia and Coconut Scallops with Papaya Cilantro Sauce

Executive Chef Luigi Baretto
Ram's Head Inn, Absecon, NJ

16 large sea scallops
1 tsp. chopped cilantro
salt and white pepper to taste
juice of 1 lime
5 oz. macadamia nuts, chopped
5 oz. shredded coconut
Papaya Cilantro Sauce (Recipe appears on page 107.)
cilantro leaves
kiwi slices

Place scallops in a bowl. Sprinkle with cilantro, salt and pepper, and lime juice. Marinate in refrigerator for 1 hour.

Preheat oven to 350°. Mix together chopped macadamia nuts and shredded coconut. Drain scallops from marinade and coat them thoroughly in the mixture.

Arrange scallops in a casserole dish. Cover with aluminum foil and bake for 10 minutes. Uncover casserole and bake for an additional 10 minutes until golden brown in color.

Heat papaya sauce over low heat until it starts to boil. Remove from fire. Spoon sauce on dish and arrange scallops on top. Garnish with cilantro leaves and slices of kiwi.

Serves 4

Grilled Sea Scallops in Boursin Cheese and Sun-dried Tomato Sauce

Executive Chef Karl L. Patton C.C.C., C.H.C.
Three Chimneys Inn, Durham, NH

2 T. olive oil
2 oz. sun-dried tomatoes, julienned
4 T. minced shallots
5 oz. heavy whipping cream
3 oz. Boursin cheese
salt and pepper to taste
3 lb. fresh jumbo sea scallops
1 T. lemon juice

In a hot skillet, heat 1 tablespoon olive oil. Sauté sun-dried tomatoes and shallots until shallots are translucent. Add heavy cream and Boursin cheese. Add salt and pepper and cook until sauce thickens. Remove from the heat.

Toss the scallops with remaining olive oil, lemon juice, salt, and pepper. Grill the scallops until the centers are no longer translucent.

Place the sauce on the bottom of each plate and top it with the grilled scallops. A further option would be to toss fresh angel hair pasta with the sauce.

Serves 4 to 6

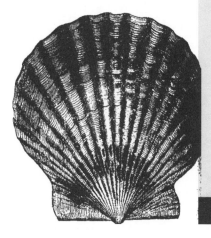

About Three Chimneys Inn

Most Known For:
hearty traditional American fare

Years in Business:
2

Most Popular Table:
in front of the fireplace

Chef:
Karl Patton

Education/Training:
Penn State

Influences:
old New England recipes

Favorite Foods:
well-marinated Porterhouse steak

Favorite Cookbooks:
On Cooking

Stuffed Shrimp Jake

Executive Chef Christopher "Jake" Brandl
Redingtons Fine Seafood Restaurant, Point Pleasant, NJ

About Redingtons Fine Seafood

Most Known For:
fine seafood

Years In Business:
13

Most Popular Table:
window table

Chef:
Christopher "Jake" Brandl

Education/Training:
Johnson & Wales University

Influences:
playing with and layering food

Hobbies:
hockey, soccer

Hometown:
Farmingdale, NJ

Favorite Foods:
blackened tuna with shiitake mushroom demi-glace and roasted garlic potatoes

Favorite Cookbook:
anything by Charlie Trotter and Emeril

4 T. butter
1 cup diced onions
2 shallots, chopped
1 lb. button mushrooms, sliced
1 lb. plum tomatoes, skinned and diced
1 lb. Calico bay scallops
1 cup sherry
2 eggs
1 cup heavy cream
4 oz. Romano cheese, grated
1 cup seasoned bread crumbs
salt and pepper to taste
16 large shrimp, cleaned and deveined, shells reserved
16 slices (about $\frac{1}{2}$ lb.) Muenster cheese
Sherry Shrimp Sauce (Recipe appears on page 104.)

In a sauté pan, melt butter over medium-high heat. Add onions, shallots, mushrooms, and tomatoes. Add bay scallops and cook about 2 minutes. Add 1 cup sherry and allow liquid to reduce so almost none remains. Add eggs and heavy cream; cook 5 minutes more. Add Romano cheese, bread crumbs, and salt and pepper. Combine well; then remove from heat and allow to cool.

Preheat oven to 375°. Lay shrimp on a greased cooking tray. Place 2 ounces of stuffing on each shrimp. Cook for 8 minutes. Remove from oven and place 1 slice of Muenster on each shrimp. Return to oven until cheese is melted, about 1 or 2 minutes.

To serve, arrange 4 shrimp on each place and nap with sherry shrimp sauce.

Serves 4

Soft-shell Crab with Thai Noodles

Owner Larry Boylan
The Inn at Sugar Hill, Mays Landing, NJ

4 soft-shell crabs
salt and pepper
1 cup flour
4 eggs, lightly beaten
$1\frac{1}{2}$ cup panko (Japanese breadcrumbs, but plain,
   unseasoned breadcrumbs will work fine)
peanut or vegetable oil
Thai Noodles (Recipe appears on page 80.)
whole basil leaves

Clean crabs. Season with salt and pepper, dredge in flour, and shake off excess. Dip in eggs and then into breadcrumbs. Heat oil (1/2") in a heavy pan. When hot (about 350°), fry crabs about 2 minutes each side. (Be careful. They sometimes have a tendency to pop when they go into the oil.) Keep warm and set aside.

   Divide Thai noodles between 4 plates. Place one crab on top of noodles and garnish with some whole basil leaves.

Serves 2 as entree
Serves 4 as appetizer

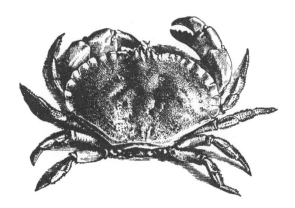

Goat Cheese and Crab Stuffed Eggplant

Executive Chef Don Dickerson
Christian's Restaurant, Chatham, MA

"Tomatoes and oregano make it Italian; wine and tarragon make it French. Sour cream makes it Russian; lemon and cinnamon make it Greek. Soy sauce makes it Chinese; garlic makes it good."

— Alice May Brock

2 medium eggplants, peeled and sliced into 16 slices
$\frac{1}{4}$ cup olive oil
$\frac{1}{4}$ cup balsamic vinegar
1 lb. goat cheese, softened
1 lb. Maine crabmeat, cartilage free
2 T. minced shallots
2 T. chopped fresh basil
8 oz. roasted garlic, pureed
2 tsp. kosher salt
2 tsp. black pepper
4 cups Basil Marinara (Recipe appears on page 106.)
8 fresh basil sprigs
$\frac{1}{2}$ lb. Parmesan cheese, shredded

Grill each eggplant slice on a hot grill. Brush or spray on oil and vinegar. Grill until eggplant is softened but not charred. Remove from grill and allow to cool.

Blend goat cheese, crabmeat, shallots, basil, garlic, salt, and pepper in mixer until consistent. Heat marinara sauce.

Preheat oven to 375°. Place a 2 ounce dollop of stuffing in the center of each eggplant slice. Roll as you would a crepe. Place stuffed eggplants (16 rolls) in an ovenproof dish and bake for 3 to 4 minutes or until cheese is oozing out of each end.

To serve, ladle about 1/2 cup marinara sauce onto each serving plate. Place one stuffed eggplant in the center of plate, horizontally. Place second eggplant vertically above the first slice to form a "T." Garnish with basil and Parmesan cheese.

Serves 8

Mushroom Crab Cakes

Chef/Partner David Graham
Van Scoy's Bistro, Cape May, NJ

1 lb. backfin, backfin-lump, or lump crabmeat
2 oz. shiitake mushrooms, stems removed
2 oz. portobello mushrooms, gills removed
2 oz. domestic mushrooms, gills removed
$\frac{1}{4}$ cup minced onion
1 T. olive oil
$1\frac{1}{2}$ T. white wine
$1\frac{1}{2}$ T. minced garlic
1 T. minced fresh basil
1 egg, beaten
$\frac{3}{8}$ cup mayonnaise
1 T. Old Bay seasoning
$\frac{1}{2}$ to 1 cup unseasoned bread crumbs
2 T. butter
Chilled Sauce Vert (Recipe appears on page 107.)

Thoroughly clean crabmeat of any shells. Set aside. Finely chop all mushrooms. Sauté mushrooms and onion in olive oil until onions are translucent. Add wine, garlic, and basil. Cook until most of the liquid evaporates. Allow mixture to cool.

When room temperature, add crabmeat, egg, mayonnaise, Old Bay, and 1/2 cup bread crumbs. Use hands to mix together thoroughly. (Mixture should be firm but not dry.) Continue to add bread crumbs until mixture reaches desired consistency. Fashion mixture into 8 cakes.

Melt butter in shallow fry pan or on griddle. Gently fry cakes at a moderate temperature until cakes are golden brown. Serve with chilled sauce vert.

Serves 2 as entree
Serves 8 as appetizer

Chef Note

For variety, coat cakes with Cajun seasoning and cook on dry griddle pan at low heat. This is called bronzing and is an ideal alternative to blackening when you do not have a commercial exhaust system.

Pastas and Risottos

Thai Noodles

Owner Larry Boylan
The Inn at Sugar Hill, Mays Landing, NJ

1 T. vegetable oil
1 medium onion, julienned
2 plum tomatoes, seeded and diced
2 cloves garlic, minced
1 tsp. yellow curry paste
1 tsp. curry powder
1 cup chicken broth
1 can coconut milk
salt and white pepper
$\frac{1}{2}$ cup packed Thai basil leaves, roughly chopped
4 scallions, thinly sliced crosswise
1 lb. linguine or spaghetti

Heat oil in sauté pan over medium-high heat. Add onions and tomatoes to pan and cook until onion is soft. Add garlic, curry paste, and curry powder; cook 1 more minute. Add broth to pan and simmer until liquid is reduced by half. Add coconut milk and reduce also by half. Season with salt and pepper to taste and stir in basil and scallions. If sauce seems too thin, you can thicken it with a little cornstarch and water. Set aside and keep warm.

In a large pot of salted water, cook pasta according to instructions. Toss cooked pasta with Thai sauce and serve alone or with soft-shell crabs. (Recipe appears on page 75.)

Serves 4

Chef Tip

Curry paste, coconut milk, and Thai basil leaves are available in most Asian food markets. Sweet basil will substitute nicely for Thai basil.

Toasted Linguine with Julienned Chicken and Sun-dried Tomatoes

Executive Chef Daniel Dogan
The Terrace at Greenhill, Wilmington, DE

2 T. olive oil
2 T. butter
2 T. minced shallot
1 tsp. minced garlic
6 oz. boneless chicken breast, cleaned and sliced into strips
flour
8 sun-dried tomatoes, julienned
4 shiitake mushroom caps, julienned
4 chanterelle mushrooms, halved
1 medium portobello mushroom, quartered
4 oz. white wine
4 oz. demi-glace
1 T. chopped fresh rosemary
1 T. chopped fresh sage
6 oz. toasted linguine
1 sprig rosemary
3 fresh sage leaves

Heat olive oil and butter in sauté pan. Add shallots and garlic and sauté until translucent. Dredge chicken strips in flour and brown on each side over medium heat. Add sun-dried tomatoes and mushrooms. Add white wine and reduce liquid by 1/2. Add demi-glace, rosemary, and sage. Toss with pasta and plate. Garnish with fresh herbs.

Serves 2

Chef Tip

To toast pasta: Lay pasta on baking pan and sprinkle with olive oil, lightly coating pasta. Place in preheated 350° oven and brown. Let cool. Then cook al dente.

Tortellini Pavarotti

Chef /Owner Joseph Massaglia
Mama Mia's Ristorante, Seaville, NJ

About Mama Mia's

Most Known For:
one and only tira misu; brown sauce

Years in Business:
11

Most Popular Table:
Tables 13 and 14

Chef:
Joseph Massaglia

Education/Training:
Villa d' Este Culinary Institute in Italy; 5 years on tourist ship

Influences:
"It's in my blood. I was raised with a pair of tongs in my hands."

Hobbies:
creating innovative food combinations, wine tasting

Hometown:
Seaville, NJ

Favorite Foods:
steak, baked potato

Favorite Cookbooks:
Italian Regional Cooking by Ada Boni, *Mama Mia's Italian Cookbook* by Angela Catanzaro

$1\frac{1}{2}$ lbs. tricolor, ricotta cheese filled tortellini
4 oz. butter
12 to 15 leaves fresh sage OR 3 oz. rubbed sage
$\frac{1}{2}$ tsp. thyme
$\frac{1}{2}$ tsp. salt
$\frac{1}{2}$ tsp. white pepper
12 oz. dry white wine
16 oz. heavy cream
1 lb. jumbo lump crabmeat
8 to 10 leaves fresh basil, finely chopped
8 oz. grated Parmesan cheese

Boil tortellini in salted water for 5 minutes or until done. Set aside.

In a large 10" or 12" saucepan, heat butter to golden brown. Add sage, thyme, salt, and pepper. Add white wine and heavy cream. Heat until liquid is reduced by half. Add cooked tortellini. Fold in crabmeat. Cook until heated through. Add fresh basil and Parmesan cheese. (If too dry, add a touch more heavy cream.)

Serves 4

Seafood Linguine

Executive Chef Frank McMullen
Wequassett Inn, Chatham, MA

2 T. butter
2 T. chopped garlic
2 T. chopped shallots
16 large shrimp, peeled and deveined
12 oz. sea scallops, side muscle removed
16 mussels, washed
$\frac{3}{4}$ cup white wine
$1\frac{1}{2}$ cups heavy cream
$\frac{1}{4}$ cup chopped basil
$\frac{1}{4}$ cup chopped sun-dried tomatoes
$\frac{3}{4}$ lb. fresh linguine pasta
salt and pepper to taste
Parmesan cheese

Heat butter in large sauté pan. Add garlic and shallots; cook 3 to 4 minutes. Add shrimp, scallops, and mussels; cook 5 to 8 minutes. Remove seafood from pan and keep warm. Add wine to pan; cook until liquid is reduced by half. Add cream and bring to a boil for 2 to 3 minutes. Add basil and sun-dried tomatoes.

In separate pot, boil linguine until tender; strain. Add seafood back to sauce in sauté pan. Add pasta. Season with salt and pepper. Serve with good Parmesan cheese.

Serves 4

About Wequassett Inn

Most Known For:
local seafood

Years In Business:
54

Most Popular Table:
window tables overlooking Pleasant Bay

Chef:
Frank McMullen

Education/Training:
Culinary Institute of America

Influences:
fresh local products

Penne and Shrimp with Vodka Sauce

Chef/Owner William C. Gomlick
Boathouse Restaurant, Bethany Beach, DE

About Boathouse Restaurant

Most Known For:
fresh seafood and pastas

Years in Business:
9

Most Popular Table:
outside porch front corner

Chef:
William Gomlick

Education/Training:
graduate of Peter Kumps N.Y. School of Cooking

Influences:
love of fishing and the outdoors

Hobbies:
surfing, hunting, skiing

Hometown:
Bethany Beach, DE

Favorite Foods:
wild game

Favorite Cookbook:
K-Paul's Fork in the Road, James Beard's American Cookery

2 T. olive oil
2 cups sliced fresh mushrooms
1 cup chopped scallions
3 oz. proscuitto, julienned
16 (U-15) shrimp, peeled and deveined
$\frac{1}{2}$ cup vodka
1 qt. heavy cream
1 cup marinara sauce
1 lb. cooked penne pasta
$\frac{1}{2}$ cup Parmesan cheese

In a sauté pan, warm olive oil over high heat. Add mushrooms, scallions, proscuitto, and shrimp; sauté about 2 minutues. Remove solids and keep warm. Add vodka to sauté pan. (Be careful, it may flame up.) Add heavy cream and marinara sauce and stir lightly to combine. Add cooked penne and reserved mixture and toss until well coated. Serve tossed with Parmesan cheese.

Serves 4

Tuscan Grain Salad

Executive Chef Rita Tyler
The Woodbox Inn, Nantucket, MA

1½ cups spelt
6 cups water
1 cucumber, peeled, seeded, and finely diced
1 cup seeded, diced tomato
2 scallions, thinly sliced
½ whole lemon, finely diced
¼ cup chopped fresh basil leaves
1 tsp. minced garlic
1 cup extra virgin olive oil
1 tsp. salt
1 tsp. freshly ground black pepper

Place spelt in a large saucepan and cover with water. Bring to a boil. Reduce heat to medium-low, simmer until tender. Drain. Cool to room temperature.

In a large bowl, combine spelt with remaining ingredients and toss well. Serve at room temperature or store covered in refrigerator for up to 3 days. If refrigerated, bring to room temperature before serving. (Wonderful when served over baby lettuces and topped with diced smoked bacon, quail eggs, and sautéed soft-shell crabs.)

Serves 6

Chef Note

Spelt is a cereal grain that has been cultivated and enjoyed by humans for 9,000 years. In Italy it is known as "farro" and is ground into flour that is used to make pasta and pizza. The cooked whole grain has a mellow, nutty flavor. Spelt is higher in protein than wheat and can be digested by people with wheat allergies.

Maryland Risotto

Executive Chef Michael Cajigao
Phillips by the Sea, Ocean City, MD

¾ cup olive oil
4 cloves garlic, chopped
1 cup diced onion
3 cups Arborio rice
1 cup dry white wine
3 cups diced canned or fresh tomatoes
pinch saffron threads
1 lb. small shrimp, peeled
1 lb. lump crabmeat, shells removed
salt and pepper to taste
grated Parmesan cheese

Bring 12 cups of water to a boil; then cover and simmer.

Heat 6 tablespoons olive oil in a large sauté pan. Add garlic and onion. Add rice and stir until coated, about 2 or 3 minutes. Add wine and tomatoes; cook until liquid is absorbed. Gradually add 1 cup of the hot water and then add saffron. As water is absorbed, continue to add hot water, 1 cup at a time, stirring constantly.

In a separate skillet, heat remaining 6 tablespoons oil. Add shrimp; cook until opaque, about 5 to 6 minutes. Add crabmeat; toss to combine. Add to rice and mix well. Add additional hot water if risotto is too tacky. Serve in bowls and season with salt and pepper and Parmesan cheese.

Serves 8 as entree

"Now in the heydey of summer,

The full, warm robust middle age of the year;

The earth, ripe with products as well as promise."

— Daniel Grayson

Lobster Risotto

Chef Russell Dare
Doris & Ed's, Highlands, NJ

$\frac{1}{2}$ cup diced onion
3 turns fresh black pepper from pepper mill
2 tsp. olive oil
$\frac{1}{2}$ cup dry white wine
1 cup Arborio rice
$3\frac{3}{4}$ cups lobster stock or clam juice
4 oz. cooked lobster meat, chopped
$\frac{1}{2}$ cup grated Parmesan cheese
3 T. sweet butter
fresh herbs (chervil, tarragon, or chives) for garnish

Season onion with pepper and sauté in olive oil until
translucent. Add white wine and reduce by two thirds. Add
rice and stir to coat. Over low flame, stir in stock, 1 cup at a
time, until absorbed. Once all stock has been added and
absorbed, add lobster meat, grated cheese, and stir. Mix in
1 tablespoon of butter at a time until creamy. (Be careful
not to overheat or butter will separate.) Serve in small
bowls or on appetizer plates and garnish with fresh herbs.

Serves 4

Sides

Chalfonte Eggplant Casserole

Chefs Dot Burton and Lucille Thompson
The Chalfonte Hotel, Cape May, NJ

5 medium eggplants, diced
6 medium onions, diced
4 (28 oz.) cans peeled tomatoes, well drained
$\frac{1}{4}$ cup Worcestershire sauce
2 tsp. salt
1 tsp. pepper
1 cup Helen's Thick Cream Sauce (Recipe appears on page 105.)
$\frac{1}{4}$ cup melted bacon grease or vegetable oil
3 T. margarine
2 T. bread crumbs
$1\frac{1}{2}$ cups freshly grated sharp cheese
paprika to taste

Simmer eggplants and onions in large pot until tender. Drain well. Add tomatoes, Worcestershire sauce, salt, and pepper. Mix in cream gravy. Stir in bacon grease and 2 tablespoons margarine.

Preheat oven to 450°. Melt remaining 1 tablespoon margarine in a 3-quart casserole dish. Sprinkle 1 table-spoon bread crumbs over margarine. Add eggplant mixture. Sprinkle remaining crumbs, cheese, and paprika over eggplant mixture. Brown in oven until heated through.

Serves 12

Chef Tip

The chefs let the tomatoes drain all morning. "Be sure and get them dry," they advise.

Spring Vegetable Strudel

Executive Chef Luigi Baretto
Ram's Head Inn, Absecon, NJ

4 sheets phyllo dough
melted butter
fresh garlic
1 lb. fresh spinach, blanched for 1 minute
salt, pepper, and Parmesan cheese to season
1 eggplant, skinned and sliced in $\frac{1}{4}$" thick pieces
2 carrots, peeled, julienned, and blanched for 3 minutes
2 zucchini, julienned
2 yellow squash, julienned
8 oz. shiitake mushrooms, sliced
1 portobello mushroom, sliced
3 red peppers, roasted, skinned, and julienned
1 sheet puff pastry dough
egg wash

Preheat oven to 350°. Brush each layer of phyllo dough with melted butter and rub with fresh garlic. Place blanched spinach atop the stacked phyllo dough and season with salt, pepper, and Parmesan cheese. Add the remaining vegetables and season again with salt, pepper, and Parmesan cheese. Roll the phyllo dough to hold all the vegetables inside and place on top of puff pastry sheet. Brush the top with egg wash. Bake 20 to 30 minutes or until golden brown. Slice into 1" thick pieces.

Serves 8

About Ram's Head Inn

Chef:
Luigi Baretto C.E.C.

Education/Training:
Italy

Influences:
local and regional foods and produce

Hobbies:
gardening

Hometown:
Absecon, NJ

Favorite Foods:
Northern Italian and Asian

Favorite Cookbook:
professional books

About Vorelli's

Most Known For:
aged steaks, dazzling entrees, extensive and innovative appetizer menu

Years in Business:
20

Chef:
Terri Vorelli is chef/owner. Bruce Penfield and Roberta Brown are also chefs at Vorelli's.

Education/Training:
Culinary Institute of America at Greystone

Influences:
the magic and excitement of food

Hobbies:
writing new recipes and reviving old ones

Favorite Foods:
French, Italian, Mediterranean, and Caribbean

Favorite Cookbook:
The Professional Chef, Classical Sauce Making, and cookbooks of ethnic origins

Roasted Vegetables

Chef/Owner Terri Vorelli
Vorelli's Restaurant, Provincetown, MA

1 cup light olive oil
1 tsp. fresh thyme
1 tsp. salt
cracked black pepper
4 red bliss potatoes, unpeeled and cut in half
4 medium white turnips, peeled and cut in half
4 medium onions, peeled and cut in half
6 carrots, peeled and cut in half

Combine oil, thyme, salt, and pepper and toss with potatoes, turnips, carrots, and onions. Roast vegetables in a 375° oven until brown and tender.

Serves 4

Potato Leek Plank

Executive Chef Luigi Baretto
Ram's Head Inn, Absecon, NJ

2 baking potatoes, julienned
1 cup leeks, julienned
1 T. flour
$\frac{1}{2}$ tsp. baking powder
salt and pepper to taste
3 egg yolks
1 cup vegetable oil plus $\frac{1}{2}$ cup for frying

Combine first 6 ingredients plus 1 cup oil in a medium bowl; mix well. Flatten mixture into oval-shaped plank approximately 5" long and 3" wide. In a heavy pan, heat about 1/2 cup oil until it sputters. Fry plank about 2 minutes on each side until golden brown and crisp around the edges. Cut into 4 pieces. Serve immediately or transfer to oven proof platter and keep warm in a 250° oven.

Serves 4

Caribbean Baked Beans

Chef/Owner Neil R. Elsohn
Waters Edge Restaurant, Cape May, NJ

1 cup dry black beans
1 T. pureed chipotle pepper in adobo sauce
2 T. dark rum (preferrably Meyers)
$\frac{1}{4}$ cup dark brown sugar
$\frac{1}{2}$ cup ketchup
$\frac{1}{2}$ cup orange juice
juice of 2 limes

Cover beans with water and soak overnight.

When ready to prepare beans, drain beans and discard soaking water. Return beans to pot, add clean water, and cook until al dente.

Preheat oven to 400°. Whisk together remaining ingredients until smooth. Stir into black beans. Bake covered for 60 minutes.

Serves 4

"A body on vacation tends to remain on vacation unless acted upon by an outside force."

— Carol Reichel

About Mews Restaurant

Most Known For:
fine food

Years in Business:
16

Chef:
Laurence deFreitas

Education/Training:
educated in Guyana, Toronto, and London

Influences:
combinations of flavors

Hobbies:
tennis, photography

Hometown:
Provincetown, MA

Favorite Foods:
Indian curries, Asian preparations

Favorite Cookbook:
anything by Madeleine Kamman

Stewed Sweet Potatoes

Executive Chef Laurence deFreitas
Mews Restaurant, Provincetown, MA

$\frac{1}{4}$ pound smoked bacon, diced
$\frac{1}{2}$ red onion, diced
2 sweet potatoes, diced
$\frac{1}{2}$ cup chopped fresh rosemary

In a sauté pan, gently cook bacon until it starts to release its oil. Add onion and cook until transparent. Add sweet potatoes and cook until tender. Add rosemary. Serve as a side dish or as part of Lobster and Sweet Potato Stew. (Recipe appears on page 39.)

Serves 2

Mashed Sweet Potatoes

Assistant Executive Chef Roger Morgan
Bally's Park Place, Atlantic City, NJ

3 large sweet potatoes, peeled and quartered
3 Idaho potatoes, peeled and quartered
$\frac{1}{2}$ cup brown sugar
4 T. salted butter
1 T. chopped fresh ginger
2 tsp. ground cinnamon
salt to taste

Place sweet potatoes and Idaho potatoes in a pot. Cover with cold water. Over medium-high heat, cook until done. Drain water and place potatoes in warm oven to dry out excess moisture. When dry, mash and combine with remaining ingredients.

Serves 4

Mashed Potatoes

Chef/Owner Fredric Byarm
Fredric's Restaurant, West Creek, NJ

2 large red bliss potatoes, peeled and diced
2 large Idaho potatoes, peeled and diced
8 oz. half-and-half
8 oz. butter
salt and pepper to taste

Boil potatoes in salted water until just cooked through. (Do not overcook.) Preheat oven to 350°. Strain potatoes and place on a baking sheet. Bake 4 to 5 minutes. Meanwhile, place half-and-half and 4 ounces butter in small saucepan over low heat. Dice remaining butter and keep cold.

   Place cooked potatoes and cold butter in food mill. Mill through. Using a wooden spoon, fold in butter and half-and-half mixture. Incorporate until velvety. Add salt and pepper to taste.

Serves 4

Potato-Spinach Pancakes

Chef Diane K. Muentz
Alexander's Inn, Cape May, NJ

About Alexander's Inn

Most Known For:
South Jersey's most beautiful dining room

Years in Business:
21

Most Popular Table:
solarium

Chef:
Diane K. Muentz

Education/Training:
The Restaurant School, Philadelphia, PA

Influences:
availability and economy

Hobbies:
making wedding cakes, antiques, politics

Hometown:
Baltimore, MD

Favorite Foods:
homemade vanilla ice cream

Favorite Cookbook:
Le Bec-Fin Recipes
by Georges Perrier

1 cup all-purpose flour, sifted
1 tsp. baking powder
1 tsp. salt
1 tsp. sugar
1 cup cooked mashed potatoes
6 oz. or $1\frac{1}{2}$ cup chopped spinach
1 egg, lightly beaten
$\frac{1}{4}$ cup melted butter
$\frac{3}{4}$ cup milk

Mix all ingredients except milk. Blend in milk slowly until a very thick batter forms. Pour 1/4 cup batter on a heated, lightly greased griddle. Brown on one side; flip with spatula. Brown on other side. Serve warm as a side with roast pork or poultry. Or for brunch, top pancakes with poached egg and hollandaise sauce.

Serves 6

Truffle Whipped Potato Profiterole

Chef/Owner David Plum
The Old Manse Inn & Restaurant, Brewster, MA

1 cup water
1 cup plus 2⅔ T. sweet butter
1 cup flour
4 eggs, beaten
6 potatoes, peeled and cut into uniform size
2 T. truffle oil
½ cup butter
1 cup heavy (use more or less to reach desired consistency)
2 T. truffle pieces
salt and white pepper to taste

Preheat oven to 400°. Combine water and sweet butter in small saucepan and bring to a boil. Stir in flour. Allow mixture to cool. When cool, add eggs and mix well. Put dough in pastry bag fitted with a round tip. Pipe small mounds onto a greased and floured nonstick sheet pan. Bake until browned, about 12 to 15 minutes.

In a medium pot, cover potatoes with cold water. Simmer until tender. Drain and whip potatoes with hand blender. Add oil, butter, heavy cream, truffle pieces, and salt and white pepper. Taste and adjust seasoning.

Split cooked profiteroles in half. Put potato mixture into pastry bag fitted with large star tip and pipe mixture onto bottom halves of profiteroles. Top with other half and serve. Great with filet mignon or roasted spring lamb chops. Devine! Sublime! Etc.!

Serves 8

About The Old Manse Inn & Restaurant

Most Known For:
creative cuisine

Years In Business:
3

Most Popular Table:
Porch #5

Chef:
David Plum

Education/Training:
CIA graduate, trained under Craig Shelton at The Ryland Inn

Influences:
cuisines of the world

Hobbies:
going to the beach

Hometown:
Brewster, MA

Favorite Foods:
homemade cheeseburgers on the BBQ

Favorite Cookbook:
Norman's New World Cuisine, From My Kitchen to Your Table by Bobby Flay

Corn Crab Confit

Chef/Owner Fredric Byarm
Fredric's Restaurant, West Creek, NJ

2 oz. butter
1 fennel bulb, julienned
1 large yellow onion, julienned
16 oz. frozen corn kernels
1 cup apple juice
2 cups white wine
2 cups white vinegar
2 cups sugar
$\frac{1}{2}$ tsp. cayenne pepper
1 lb. Phillips blue crabmeat (jumbo lump)
1 T. minced fresh parsley

In a small sauté pan, add 1 ounce butter, fennel, and onion.
Cook until onions are translucent. Heat a separate pan over
high heat. Add corn and remaining butter. Brown corn; then
add to fennel and onion mixture. Add apple juice, wine,
white vinegar, sugar, and cayenne pepper. Cook over
medium heat until liquid evaporates. Strain. Fold crabmeat
and parsley into mixture. Serve hot.

Serves 4

"Give me the
luxuries of life
and I will willingly
do without the
necessities."

— Frank Lloyd
Wright

Fagioli All'Olio

Centro's creative kitchen staff
Centro Ristorante & Bar, Darien, CT

2 sweet Italian sausage links, cooked and sliced on a bias
1 bulb fennel, diced
2 tsp. chopped garlic
$\frac{1}{4}$ cup extra virgin olive oil
$\frac{1}{2}$ cup cooked cannelloni beans
$\frac{1}{2}$ cup cooked butter beans
$\frac{1}{2}$ cup cooked pink beans
$\frac{1}{2}$ cup cooked pinto beans
salt and pepper to taste
3 to 4 bunches arugula
fresh lemon slices

Sauté sliced sausage, fennel, garlic, and olive oil. Add
beans and salt and pepper and cook until heated through.
Add additional olive oil if desired.

Serve over arugula and garnish with fresh lemon slices.

Serves 4

Sauces, Salsas, and Such

Game Sauce

Executive Chef Luigi Baretto
Ram's Head Inn, Absecon, NJ

3 lbs. venison bones and trims
1 carrot, sliced
1 celery stalk, sliced
$\frac{1}{2}$ medium onion, sliced
1 bay leaf
$\frac{1}{2}$ tsp. fresh thyme
$\frac{1}{2}$ tsp. cracked black pepper
2 to 3 juniper berries
1 T. butter
1 T. heavy cream
1 T. red currant jelly

Roast bones in a 375° oven until they are brown in color. Transfer bones to a large stock pot. Add 4 quarts water and bring to a boil. Add vegetables, spices, and juniper berries. Simmer for approximately 3 hours. Strain. Return stock to pot and bring to a boil. Whisk in butter, heavy cream, and jelly. Check seasonings. Serve immediately or refrigerate.

"The discovery of a new dish does more for human happiness than the discovery of a new star."

— Anthelme Brillat-Savarin, *The Physiology of Taste*

Seafood Sauce

Director of Culinary Services Ralph J. Coughenour
Acorns Restaurant at the New England Conference Center
Durham, NH

$5\frac{1}{2}$ T. butter
$3\frac{1}{2}$ T. flour
$\frac{2}{3}$ cup light cream or half-and-half
$3\frac{1}{2}$ T. diced mushrooms
2 T. minced shallot
3 T. grated Swiss cheese
$\frac{1}{4}$ tsp. Worcestershire sauce
$\frac{2}{3}$ tsp. dry mustard
salt and white pepper to taste
$3\frac{1}{2}$ T. dry white wine
2 tsp. fresh lemon juice
3 T. mayonnaise

Melt $3\frac{1}{2}$ tablespoons butter in a saucepan. Add flour and cook, being careful not to let mixture burn. Whip in light cream or half-and-half and simmer 5 minutes.

In a separate pan, sauté mushrooms and shallots in remaining butter until just done. Add to sauce. Add cheese, Worcestershire sauce, mustard, and salt and pepper. Remove from heat. Stir in wine, lemon juice and mayonnaise.

Sherry Shrimp Sauce

Executive Chef Christopher "Jake" Brandl
Redingtons Fine Seafood Restaurant, Point Pleasant, NJ

2 tsp. butter
$\frac{1}{4}$ cup chopped shallots
$\frac{1}{4}$ cup chopped garlic
$\frac{1}{4}$ cup chopped onions
shrimp shells from 1 lb. shrimp
1 cup sherry
2 T. flour
heavy cream
salt and pepper to taste

In a sauté pan, melt butter over medium-high heat. Add shallots, garlic, onions, and shrimp shells; sauté for about 10 minutes. Add sherry and cook until liquid is reduced by half. Add flour and cook for 5 minutes, stirring so it does not burn. Add cream and salt and pepper. Simmer for 10 minutes. Strain and keep warm. Serve over seafood dishes, pasta, or Stuffed Shrimp Jake (Recipe appears on page 74.)

"Vacation used to be a luxury, however, in today's world, it has become a necessity."

— Unknown

Helen's Thick Cream Sauce

Chefs Dot Burton and Lucille Thompson
The Chalfonte Hotel, Cape May, NJ

3 T. butter
$\frac{1}{2}$ cup flour
1 cup milk (heated) or light cream
salt
fresh ground pepper

Melt butter in heavy-bottomed saucepan. Stir in flour and cook, stirring constantly for 2 minutes or until the paste bubbles a bit. Add hot milk. Bring to a boil, stirring as sauce thickens. Add salt and pepper to taste. Lower heat and continue stirring for 2 to 3 more minutes until sauce is very thick. Remove from heat. (If you'd like to cool this sauce for later use, cover with wax paper or pour a film of milk over it to prevent skin from forming.)

Yields 1 cup

About The Chalfonte Hotel

Most Known For:
Southern style cooking

Years in Business:
123(!)

Chefs:
Dot Burton and Lucille Thompson

Education/Training:
50 years cooking at the Chalfonte

Influences:
Southern heritage

Hobbies:
family, church activities

Hometown:
West Cape May, NJ

Favorite Foods:
what they cook!

Favorite Cookbook:
Their mother's — *I Just Quit Stirrin' When the Tastin's Good*

Basil Marinara Sauce

Executive Chef Don Dickerson
Christian's Restaurant, Chatham, MA

$\frac{1}{2}$ cup olive oil
$\frac{1}{2}$ cup minced garlic
$\frac{1}{2}$ cup minced shallots
1 cup chopped fresh basil
1 cup chablis
2 tsp. granulated garlic
2 T. chopped fresh parsley
$\frac{1}{2}$ T. cracked black pepper
1 T. kosher salt
1 qt. tomato sauce (Heinz is fine.)
2 qts. crushed tomatoes (I like Sclafani.)
12 plum tomatoes, parboiled and peeled

Heat oil in a large stock pot. Add garlic, shallots, and basil. Sauté until shallots are soft. Add wine and heat until liquid is reduced by half. Add all seasonings and mix well. Add all tomato products and mix well. Simmer for 2 hours.

Yields 1 gallon

Chilled Sauce Vert

Executive Chef David Graham
Van Scoy's Bistro, Cape May, NJ

2 T. white vinegar
$\frac{3}{4}$ cup Dijon mustard
$\frac{1}{4}$ cup coarsely chopped onion
$\frac{1}{3}$ lb. fresh spinach leaves, well washed and stemmed
1 oz. fresh basil, well washed and stemmed
$\frac{1}{2}$ bunch parsley leaves, well washed and stemmed
1 tsp. salt
1 tsp. ground black pepper
$2\frac{1}{2}$ cups mayonnaise

Place vinegar, mustard, and onion in blender or food processor. Liquify. Gradually add spinach, basil, parsley, salt, and pepper. Puree. In a large mixing bowl, thoroughly mix puree and mayonnaise. Refrigerate. Can be stored in refrigerator for up to 1 month.

Yields 1 quart

Chef Tip

Sauce vert is a flavorful alternative to tartar sauce and a perfect complement to spicy seafood such as blackened catfish or bronzed mushroom crab cakes. It is also a very popular salad dressing.

Papaya Cilantro Sauce

Executive Chef Luigi Baretto
Ram's Head Inn, Absecon, NJ

1 medium fresh papaya, peeled and seeded
$\frac{1}{4}$ cup water (approximate)
$\frac{1}{2}$ tsp. chopped cilantro
juice of $\frac{1}{2}$ lime
$\frac{1}{2}$ tsp. chopped jalapeño chile
$\frac{1}{4}$ tsp. ginger powder
1 oz. dark rum
salt and white pepper

Puree papaya in food processor, adding water. Pour into a saucepan and add remaining ingredients. Slowly bring to a boil over low heat. Serve hot.

Black Bean Sauce

Owner Larry Boylan
The Inn at Sugar Hill, Mays Landing, NJ

1 T. vegetable oil
1 medium onion, diced
2 cloves garlic, minced
1 tsp. ground cumin
$\frac{1}{2}$ tsp. red pepper flakes (more or less as to your heat liking)
1 T. soy sauce
1 (15 to 16 oz.) can black beans
1 (15 oz.) can chicken broth
salt and pepper

Heat oil in heavy saucepan over medium-high heat. Add onions and garlic and cook until onion is soft (do not burn the garlic). Add remaining ingredients and simmer for 15 minutes. Place in blender or food processor and puree until smooth.

Szechuan Vinaigrette

Chef/Owner Neil R. Elsohn
Waters Edge Restaurant, Cape May, NJ

$\frac{1}{4}$ cup roasted sesame oil
$\frac{1}{4}$ cup vegetable oil
2 T. sesame seeds
1 bunch scallions, minced
1 T. crushed red pepper
2 T. minced ginger
$\frac{1}{4}$ cup peanut butter
1 cup red vinegar
1 cup sugar
2 cups soy sauce

Heat oils. Add sesame seeds, scallions, red pepper, and ginger and sauté briefly. Add peanut butter, vinegar, sugar, and soy sauce. Bring to a boil. Remove from heat and chill before serving.

Jersey Tomato and Corn Relish

Owner Larry Boylan
The Inn at Sugar Hill, Mays Landing, NJ

1½ cups seeded and finely diced Jersey plum tomatoes
4 to 6 ears Jersey sweet corn, roasted, kernels cut from cob
1 medium red onion, finely diced
2 cloves garlic, minced
¼ cup chopped cilantro leaves
3 T. balsamic vinegar
½ cup extra virgin olive oil
salt and pepper to taste

Mix all ingredients together in a mixing bowl. Serve chilled or at room temperature.

Chef Tip

Roast the corn in its husk on top of a hot grill or in a hot oven (approximately 425°) for 15 to 20 minutes. The more brown the husk, the more prominent the roasted, nutty flavor will be.

Pumpkin Relish

Executive Chef Chris Hubert
The Ebbitt Room, Cape May, NJ

1 cup blanched diced pumpkin
¼ cup diced yellow and red peppers
¼ cup diced red onion
2 T. minced scallions
1 tsp. minced garlic
½ T. chopped parsley
½ T. chopped tarragon
¼ cup sugar
2 T. rice wine vinegar
4 T. olive oil
cracked black pepper to taste

In small mixing bowl, toss together pumpkin, peppers, onion, scallions, garlic, parsley, tarragon, and sugar. Add vinegar and oil. Season with black pepper to taste. Refrigerate overnight.

Mary's Salsa

Chef/Owner Mary McCabe
Bridges Restaurant on the Bay, Ocean City, NJ

Chef Note

In the summer, add melon or papaya. Zucchini, yellow squash, carrot, celery, and cooked corn can also be added.

$\frac{1}{4}$ cup EACH chopped yellow, red, orange, and green peppers
$\frac{1}{4}$ cup chopped tomato
$\frac{1}{4}$ cup chopped onion
$\frac{1}{4}$ cup chopped scallion
3 cloves garlic, chopped
$\frac{1}{4}$ cup chopped parsley
$\frac{1}{4}$ cup chopped cilantro
juice of $\frac{1}{2}$ lime
1 T. cumin
$\frac{1}{3}$ T. sea salt

Mix all ingredients together. Store covered in refrigerator.

Serves 6 to 8

Roasted Corn Salsa

Owner Larry Boylan
The Inn at Sugar Hill, Mays Landing, NJ

$1\frac{1}{2}$ cups seeded and finely diced plum tomatoes
4 to 6 ears sweet corn, roasted and kernels cut from cobs
1 medium red onion, finely diced
1 red pepper, seeded and finely diced
1 poblano pepper OR 1 green bell plus 1 jalapeño, both seeded and finely diced
2 cloves garlic, minced
$\frac{1}{4}$ cup roughly chopped cilantro leaves
juice of 2 limes
$\frac{1}{2}$ cup olive oil
1 tsp. salt
$\frac{1}{2}$ tsp. pepper
$\frac{1}{2}$ tsp. ground cumin

Mix all ingredients together in a mixing bowl. Served chilled or at room temperature.

Tomato Basil Jam

Chef Alex Mazzocca
Martin House Restaurant, Provincetown, MA

5 plum tomatoes, seeded and chopped
2 T. chopped red onion
$\frac{1}{2}$ cup sugar
$\frac{1}{4}$ tsp. cayenne pepper
3 T. tomato juice
2 T. julienned basil

Combine all ingredients but basil in a saucepan and bring to a boil. Lower heat and simmer until reduced and thickened. Add basil. Simmer 5 minutes more. Cool before serving.

Apple Chutney

Chef Gary Caron
The Dolphin Striker Restaurant, Portsmouth, NH

1 small red onion, minced
2 cloves garlic, crushed
$\frac{1}{4}$ cup balsamic vinegar
$\frac{1}{4}$ cup molasses
$\frac{1}{2}$ T. grated fresh ginger
$\frac{1}{2}$ T. salt
1 tsp. ground cloves
1 tsp. allspice
$\frac{1}{4}$ tsp. cayenne pepper
5 apples, peeled, cored, and diced into $\frac{1}{2}$" pieces
$\frac{1}{2}$ cup dried red currants
$\frac{1}{2}$ cup chopped green onion
$\frac{1}{4}$ cup pink peppercorns

Combine first 9 ingredients in a non-reactive saucepan. Heat and allow liquid to reduce by two thirds. Add apples. Cook until tender. Remove from heat. Stir in currants, green onion, and peppercorns.

Chef Note

May be served warm or cold as a side dish or accompaniment to a main course. The flavors work very well with game, but also compliment pork and fowl.

Serves 6 to 8

Sweet Stuff

Chocolate Luv Cake

Chef/Owner/Innkeeper Vivian Barry
Barry's Gull Cottage B&B, Dewey Beach, DE

4 eggs
1 cup water
$\frac{1}{2}$ cup canola oil
$\frac{1}{3}$ cup bourbon
1 box chocolate cake mix
1 box instant chocolate pudding
1 package semi-sweet chocolate chips

Preheat oven to 350°. Mix all ingredients except chocolate chips. Pour batter into greased bundt pan. Sprinkle chocolate chips over batter — do not mix in. Bake for 40 to 50 minutes or until an inserted toothpick comes out dry. Let stand in pan until cool. When cool, remove from pan, sprinkle with powered sugar, and serve with a glass of cold milk or an espresso.

Cream Cheese Pound Cake

Innkeeper Joan Wells
The Queen Victoria, Cape May, NJ

8 oz. cream cheese
¾ lb. butter
6 eggs
1 tsp. vanilla
3 cups sugar
3 cups flour

Let cream cheese, eggs, and butter come to room temperature.

Preheat oven to 325°. Mix cream cheese and butter thoroughly. Add eggs, one at a time, and mix well. Add vanilla. In a separate bowl, sift flour and sugar together. Add a small amount at a time to creamed mixture until thoroughly combined.

Spray a bundt or tube pan with nonstick pan coating; then dust with flour. Spread dough in pan and bake 90 minutes or until tester comes out clean. Cool cake 15 minutes in pan before removing. Cut into thin slices and serve plain or with fruit sauce or summer fruits.

Serves 16 to 20

Sambuca Ricotta Cake

Chef/Owner Francesco Buto
Il Pescature, Ocean City, NJ

About Il Pescature

Most Known For:
seafood

Years in Business:
3

Most Popular Table:
#11 by the fireplace

Chef: Francesco Buto

Education/Training:
The Restaurant
School, Philadelphia

Influences:
love of food and
cuisines of the world

Hobbies:
herb gardening

Hometown:
Sicily, Italy

Favorite Foods:
pastas, fish

Favorite Cookbooks:
Italian Kitchen by
Marcella Hazan,
*From the Earth to the
Table* by John Ash

6 T. butter
$\frac{3}{4}$ cup granulated sugar
$\frac{1}{3}$ cup ricotta cheese
3 large eggs, separated
$1\frac{1}{2}$ cups flour
$\frac{1}{4}$ cup sambuca
$1\frac{1}{2}$ tsp. baking powder
confectioners' sugar

Preheat oven to 350°. Grease a 9" round cake pan or springform pan. Line bottom with circle of waxed paper. Grease and flour paper; set aside.

Cream butter and sugar together til smooth. Beat in ricotta. Beat in egg yolks one at a time. Add 2 tablespoons flour and sambuca.

In a separate bowl, sift baking powder and combine with remaining flour. Combine wet and dry ingredients and stir until well blended. In another bowl, beat egg whites into stiff peaks. Fold whites into batter in thirds.

Pour batter into prepared pan. Bake for 45 minutes or until a toothpick inserted in center of cake comes out clean. Allow cake to cool for 10 minutes before turning out onto a cooling rack. Before serving, dust the cake generously with confectioners' sugar.

Serves 6 to 8

Strawberry Almond Torte

Executive Chef Cynthia Sikes
Galaxy Bar & Grille, Ocean City, MD

2 cups sugar
1 cup butter
4 eggs
1 T. almond extract
1 cup buttermilk
3 cups self-rising flour
$\frac{1}{2}$ tsp. baking powder
$\frac{1}{2}$ cup finely chopped almonds
2 pts. strawberries
$\frac{1}{2}$ cup butterscotch liqueur
fresh whipped cream

Preheat oven to 325°. Grease a 9" springform pan.

Cream together sugar, butter, and eggs. In a separate bowl, mix together extract and buttermilk. In another bowl, mix together flour, baking powder, and almonds. Alternately, add buttermilk mixture and flour mixture to sugar mixture. Mix for 3 minutes.

Pour into prepared pan and bake for 75 minutes until golden brown. Cool fully.

Slice 1 pint strawberries and soak in 1/4 cup liqueur. Place whole strawberries in another bowl and soak in remaining liqueur.

Cut cake in half, horizontally; set top aside. Put a thin layer of sliced strawberries on the bottom half of the cake. Top with a layer of whipped cream; then another layer of strawberries. Drizzle remaining juices over strawberries. Cover with top of cake. Decorate with whole strawberries and whipped cream.

About Galaxy Bar & Grille

Most Known For:
unique presentations

Years in Business:
5

Most Popular Table:
corner table

Chef:
Cynthia Sikes

Education/Training:
Johnson & Wales University

Influences:
keeping up on current trends and creating our own trends

Hobbies:
pets, swimming, musical instruments

Hometown:
Burriville, RI

Favorite Foods:
Buffalo wings with ranch dressing

Favorite Cookbook:
anything by David Burke or Bobby Flay

Sauce Sabayon with Fresh Berries

Executive Chef Fredric Link
Rose Garden Restaurant in Bar Harbor Hotel-Bluenose Inn
Bar Harbor, ME

4 egg yolks
$\frac{1}{2}$ cup sugar
$\frac{1}{3}$ cup Marsala wine
1 pt. whipped cream
$\frac{1}{2}$ pt. EACH fresh strawberries, blueberries, raspberries, blackberries

Fill a small saucepan three quarters full with water; bring to a boil. In a small stainless steel bowl, combine yolks, sugar, and wine. Place the bowl over the pot. Using a wire whisk, beat the mixture until thick and frothy. Remove bowl from the heat every 15 seconds and check for consistency. (If left on the heat too long, the eggs will overcook.) Periodically check the wire whisk to see if it's steaming — this is a sure sign that the mixture is ready. When finished, cool the mixture in refrigerator.

Using a rubber spatula, slowly incorporate whipped cream into egg mixture until fully blended. Refrigerate until ready to serve.

To serve, put berries into the mixture and slowly mix until berries are covered with sauce. Dish into 4 bowls.

Serves 4

"It's hot! I can't get cool.

I've drunk a quantity of lemonade.

I think I'll take my shoes off

And sit around in the shade."

— Shel Silverstein,
A Light in the Attic

Blackberry Cobbler

Innkeeper Joan Wells
The Queen Victoria, Cape May, NJ

3 T. cornstarch
$\frac{3}{8}$ cup water or fruit juice
1 cup plus 1 T. sugar
6 cups fresh blackberries, washed
2 T. lemon juice
$\frac{1}{2}$ tsp. cinnamon
6 T. butter, softened
2 cups flour
$2\frac{1}{2}$ tsp. baking powder
1 tsp. salt
$\frac{3}{4}$ cup milk or cream
cinnamon and sugar

Mix cornstarch with water or juice until smooth. Blend in 1 cup sugar. Season fruit with lemon juice and cinnamon. Add cornstarch mixture and let stand 15 minutes. Spray 9x13" baking dish with nonstick pan coating. Pour fruit into dish. Dot with 2 tablespoons butter.

Preheat oven to 425°. Mix together flour, baking powder, salt, and remaining sugar. Cut remaining butter into dry ingredients. Add milk or cream. Knead lightly for 30 seconds. Pat and shape to fit on top of berries. Sprinkle with cinnamon and sugar. Bake for 30 minutes, until lightly browned and fruit is bubbling. Serve warm with heavy cream if desired.

Serves 10 to 12

Harry's Crème Brûlée

Executive Chef David Leo Banks
Harry's Savoy Grill, Wilmington, DE

2 cups heavy whipping cream
$\frac{1}{4}$ cup granulated sugar
4 egg yolks
1 T. vanilla extract
$\frac{3}{4}$ cup granulated sugar (approximate)
$\frac{3}{4}$ cup brown sugar (approximate)

Preheat oven to 325°. Prepare a hot water bath for 4 (6 ounce) ramekins. Combine the cream and sugar in the top of a double boiler or in a saucepan over low heat. Heat to approximately 170°. Stir with a whip initially to combine cream and sugar; do not whip to froth.

In a small bowl, whisk the egg yolks. When cream/sugar mixture has reached desired temperature, whisk some of the hot mixture into the yolks to "temper" the yolks. Add a little at a time; stir with a whisk but do not froth. Return to hot cream/sugar mixture. Stir in the vanilla extract. Strain this mixture through a fine sieve. Skim air bubbles from top of custard mixture. Divide mixture evenly among the 4 ramekins; use a pitcher for this step.

Place ramekins in the hot water bath. Bake for approximately 30 minutes. DO NOT ALLOW WATER IN WATER BATH TO BOIL! Turn pan and allow to bake for approximately 15 minutes more. Remove ramekins from water bath and allow to cool. Refrigerate. Custard will firm up nicely under refrigeration.

Combine the topping sugars. Spread an even layer over the top of each ramekin. Heat under a hot broiler until sugar caramelizes.

Serves 4

White Chocolate Mousse with Raspberry Sauce

Innkeeper/Owner Mark Kulkowitz
The Mad Batter Restaurant at The Carroll Villa Hotel
Cape May, NJ

3 egg whites
6 to 7 T. sugar
1 cup heavy cream
$\frac{1}{4}$ lb. white chocolate, chopped
$\frac{1}{2}$ pt. raspberries
$\frac{1}{4}$ cup water

Whip egg whites until soft peaks form. Add 4 tablespoons sugar; beat until stiff peaks form. In separate bowl, whip heavy cream until stiff. Fold together egg whites, whipped cream, and chopped chocolate.

Combine remaining sugar, raspberries, and water in saucepan. Cook over low heat until berries begin to lose color. Remove from heat, puree, and strain. Return to heat and continue cooking until sauce is slightly thickened. Cool and serve with mousse.

Serves 4 to 6

> "Steep thyself in a bowl of summertime."
>
> — Virgil

Apple Bread Pudding

Innkeeper/Owner Sue H. Carroll
Mainstay Inn, Cape May, NJ

1 (1 lb.) loaf firm raisin bread, sliced and crusts removed
$\frac{1}{4}$ cup butter
3 cups peeled and sliced tart apple (3 medium apples)
2 T. all-purpose flour
$\frac{1}{2}$ cup sugar
1 tsp. ground cinnamon
4 eggs, lightly beaten
$2\frac{1}{2}$ cups milk
$\frac{1}{2}$ tsp. salt
maple syrup

If you plan to bake this dish immediately, preheat oven to 350°. Grease a 13x9x2" glass baking dish.

Cut bread slices into 3/4" cubes. Melt butter in a medium frying pan. Add apples and cook, stirring occasionally, for 5 minutes or until tender.

Combine flour, 2 tablespoons sugar, and cinnamon and stir into apples. Cook, stirring gently, for 1 minute or until thickened. Spoon into prepared baking dish. Layer the bread crumbs over apple mixture.

In a medium bowl, mix the eggs, milk, salt, and remaining sugar. Pour over bread cubes. Using a spoon, press down on the bread so it absorbs the egg mixture. May be baked immediately but best if covered and refrigerated for at least 8 hours or overnight.

Bake for 50 to 70 minutes or until golden and a knife inserted in the center comes out clean. Cut into squares and serve warm with maple syrup.

Serves 8

The Earl of Bread Puddin'

Owner Chuck Armstrong
East Bay Crab and Grille, Egg Harbor Twp., NJ

1 loaf Texas toast
$1\frac{1}{2}$ cups light brown sugar
2 T. cinnamon
10 oz. butter
4 large eggs
$\frac{3}{4}$ cup granulated sugar
pinch of nutmeg
$\frac{1}{4}$ cup vanilla extract
$1\frac{1}{4}$ cups milk
4 oz. raisins
2 cups all-purpose flour
Puddin' Sauce (see recipe)

Preheat oven to 325°. Cut crust off bread; then cut each slice in half and lay on baking sheet. Combine 1/2 cup light brown sugar and 1 tablespoon cinnamon; sprinkle over bread. Melt 6 ounces butter and drizzle over bread. Bake 15 minutes.

Increase oven temperature to 375°. Hand whip eggs. Mix in granulated sugar, remaining cinnamon, nutmeg, and vanilla. Bring milk to a boil; then slowly incorporate it into the egg mixture. Loosely lay out bread in a 9x11x2" glass baking dish. Sprinkle on raisins. Pour egg/milk mixture over bread and let stand for 5 minutes. Cover and bake for 30 minutes.

Meanwhile, mix together remaining brown sugar, remaining butter (melted), and flour. Spread on top of cooked bread pudding and bake uncovered for 20 more minutes. Let pudding cool completely before serving. Top with puddin' sauce and serve at room temperature or reheated.

Serves 8 to 10

Puddin' Sauce

1 pint heavy cream
$\frac{1}{2}$ cup sugar
4 large eggs
2 T. vanilla extract

Heat cream to a simmer, stirring constantly. Combine sugar, eggs, and vanilla; add to cream. Heat over medium heat, stirring constantly, until desired thickness is reached. Can be served hot or cold.

Nutty Rum Banana Ice Cream

Executive Chef Kenneth W. Koon
Woody's Restaurant, Rehoboth Beach, DE

"Get your ice cream. Toostie-fruitsie ice cream."

— Chico Marx in "A Day at the Races"

4 bananas
1 cup milk
$\frac{1}{2}$ cup dark rum
1 cup sugar
dash of salt
1 cup half-and-half
2 cups heavy whipping cream
$1\frac{1}{2}$ tsp. vanilla extract
$\frac{1}{2}$ cup chopped hazelnuts

Preheat oven to 350°. Cook bananas in peels on cookie sheet for 40 minutes.

Remove peels from bananas. Combine milk and rum in a saucepan. Heat over medium-high heat until bubbles form around the edges. Add hot bananas. Remove from heat and add sugar and salt. Stir until dissolved completely. Stir in half-and-half and whipping cream. Chill completely. Add vanilla and hazelnuts. Freeze in ice cream maker according to manufacturer's directions.

Serves 8

Honey Crepes

Head Chef Wayne Cousins
Norumbega Inn, Camden, ME

$1\frac{1}{2}$ cups all-purpose flour
1 T. sugar
$\frac{1}{2}$ tsp. baking powder
$\frac{1}{2}$ tsp. salt
2 cups milk
2 T. margarine or butter, melted
$\frac{1}{2}$ tsp. vanilla
2 eggs
Honey Filling (see recipe)
powdered sugar

Mix flour, sugar, baking powder, and salt in a $1\frac{1}{2}$-quart bowl. Stir in remaining ingredients, except filling and powdered sugar. Beat with wire whisk until smooth.

Lightly butter 6" to 8" skillet; heat over medium heat until bubbly. For each crepe, pour a scant 1/4 cup of batter into skillet. Immediately rotate skillet until film covers bottom. Cook until light brown. Run wide spatula around edge to loosen; flip and cook other side until light brown. Stack crepes, placing waxed paper between each. Keep covered.

Spread a thin layer of filling on warm crepes. Roll up and sprinkle with powdered sugar.

Yields 12 crepes

Honey Filling

8 oz. cream cheese
$\frac{1}{3}$ cup honey
$\frac{1}{2}$ cup sour cream
$\frac{1}{2}$ tsp. vanilla extract
zest of 1 orange

Whip cream cheese. Add remaining ingredients. Mix until creamy.

Fudge Melt-a-Ways

Owner Lorie Whissell
Angel of the Sea, Cape May, NJ

$\frac{3}{4}$ cup butter
$2\frac{1}{2}$ squares unsweetened chocolate
$\frac{1}{4}$ cup granulated sugar
2 cups graham cracker crumbs
$\frac{1}{2}$ cup chopped nuts
1 cup coconut
2 tsp. vanilla
1 egg, beaten
1 T. milk or cream
2 cups sifted powdered sugar

In a saucepan, melt 1/2 cup butter and 1 square of chocolate. Add granulated sugar, graham crumbs, nuts, coconut, 1 teaspoon vanilla, and egg to the chocolate mixture. Mix well and press into an ungreased 9x13" baking dish. Refrigerate.

Mix together remaining butter and vanilla, milk, and powdered sugar. Spread over crumb mixture. Chill.

Melt remaining chocolate and spread over chilled filling. Chill. Cut into squares before firm.

Makes 24 squares

Hazel Scented Chocolate Truffles

Chef Gary Caron
The Dolphin Striker Restaurant, Portsmouth, NH

8 oz. semi-sweet chocolate, chopped
2 oz. bittersweet chocolate, chopped
$\frac{1}{4}$ cup espresso or strong coffee, hot
scant $\frac{1}{4}$ cup hazelnut liqueur
5 oz. unsalted butter, cut into cubes
$\frac{1}{4}$ cup confectioners' sugar
$\frac{1}{4}$ cup cocoa powder
$\frac{1}{4}$ cup ground hazelnuts

Combine chopped chocolate and hot espresso in a stainless steel bowl. Place bowl over a pot of hot but not boiling water and allow chocolate to melt slowly.

When more than three quarters of chocolate is melted, add liqueur. Continue heating until mixture is melted smooth. Remove from heat and add cubed butter, a few pieces at a time. Use a rubber spatula to fold in butter until fully incorporated. Chill until fully set, about 4 to 6 hours.

In a small bowl, combine sugar, cocoa, and ground hazelnuts. Using a melon baller or sorbet scoop, form chocolate mixture into balls. Roll balls in hazelnut mixture to coat. Serve with fresh fruit or berry puree. Store in refrigerator.

Serves 6 to 8

About The Dolphin Striker

Most Known For:
chef's daily specials, seasonal creations, historic site

Years in Business:
25

Chef: Gary Caron

Education/Training:
Culinary Arts Degree, 1983

Influences:
using classical preparations with updated style

Hobbies:
making custom cutlery

Favorite Foods:
ethnic foods with plenty of heat

Breakfast

Apple and Brie Omelet Marlborough

Owner Al Hammond
The Marlborough, Woods Hole, MA

$1\frac{1}{2}$ T. butter
$\frac{1}{4}$ medium-size Granny Smith apple, peeled and thinly sliced
$\frac{1}{8}$ tsp. grated nutmeg
1 tsp. granulated sugar
1 T. brown sugar
1 T. chopped walnuts
3 eggs, whisked until foamy
6 ($\frac{1}{2}$") cubes Brie cheese

In a heavy skillet, melt 1/2 tablespoon butter. Sauté apples in butter until slightly translucent but not mushy. Sprinkle apples with nutmeg and granulated sugar. Remove apples from pan and set aside.

Mix together brown sugar and walnuts; set aside. Melt remaining butter in skillet, heating until bubbly. Pour eggs gently into bubbling butter. As eggs begin to set, lift edges to let the uncooked liquid run under. When the eggs are almost set, turn heat off. Put Brie on one half of the omelet. Top with sautéed apples and fold omelet in half. Let sit 3 to 4 minutes to allow Brie to melt. Remove to warmed plate and sprinkle with brown sugar topping.

Serves 1

Breakfast Casserole

Owner Elsie Collins
1880 House, Westhampton Beach, NY

1 lb. pork or turkey breakfast sausage
$\frac{1}{2}$ lb. sharp Cheddar cheese, grated
$\frac{1}{2}$ tsp. dry mustard
$\frac{1}{2}$ tsp. paprika
1 tsp. salt
1 cup sour cream
10 to 16 eggs (depending on desired number of servings)

Preheat oven to 325°. In large skillet, cook and crumble sausage; then drain. Coat a 2- or 3-quart dish with nonstick cooking spray. Sprinkle half of the grated cheese in bottom of the baking dish. Combine mustard, paprika, and salt with sour cream. Add in sausage and then spread mixture over grated cheese. Beat eggs and pour over mixture. Sprinkle remaining grated cheese on top. Bake 25 to 30 minutes or until set.

Serves 6 to 14

"How do like your eggs?"

— Sally Field in "Murphy's Romance"

Chicken Hash with Shiitake-Cheddar Cheese Muffins

Executive Chef Carl V. Colucci
Le Palais, Resorts Casino, Atlantic City, NJ

$1\frac{1}{2}$ T. butter
2 scallions, white part only, minced
1 leek, minced
1 lb. boneless chicken breast, diced
$\frac{1}{2}$ red bell pepper, chopped
1 T. chopped fresh thyme
$\frac{1}{2}$ tsp. black pepper
1 tsp. salt (optional)
2 T. flour
2 cups milk, warmed
$\frac{1}{2}$ cup sour cream
Shiitake-Cheddar Cheese Muffins (Recipe appears on
    page 141.)
chopped scallion green for garnish

Melt butter in a pot. Add scallions, leek, chicken, and red pepper and cook until chicken is thoroughly done. Season with thyme and black pepper. Add flour and cook 1 minute. Stir warmed milk into hash and cook for 10 minutes over low heat. Add sour cream; cook 1 minute.

Cut 4 muffins in half and put 2 halves on each plate. Serve hash over muffins and garnish with scallion greens. Hash can also be served with steamed vegetables for a delicious dinner.

Serves 4

Chef Tip

To me, one of the best parts of the day is waking up early, doing some exercise and/or chores, then sitting at the dining table to enjoy a wholesome breakfast or lunch. Here is one of those wonderful dishes that can be done ahead of time and binga, banga, booom! You're on your way!

Corn Cakes with Smoked Salmon and Crème Fraîche

Owner/Innkeeper Kim O'Mahoney
The Inn at Portsmouth Harbor, Kittery, ME

1 cup water

1 cup yellow corn meal

4 T. butter, cut into small pieces

1 cup unbleached white flour (I always use King Arthur
   Flour from Norwich, Vermont — it's the best!)

$1\frac{1}{2}$ tsp. baking powder

3 T. sugar

3 extra large eggs, beaten

1 cup milk (Nonfat works fine.)

4 scallions, thinly sliced

1 cup corn kernels (If using frozen, defrost and drain well.)
   vegetable oil

$\frac{1}{3}$ lb. smoked salmon, thinly sliced

Crème Fraîche (see recipe)

sliced scallions and/or chives

Bring water to a boil. Place corn meal in large bowl and cover with boiling water. Add butter and set aside as butter melts. In a separate bowl, blend flour, baking powder, and sugar. In a smaller bowl, combine eggs, milk, scallions, and corn. When the cornmeal is cool, add the egg mixture and stir with a spatula until smooth. Add dry ingredients and blend well.

   Heat oven to 200°. Heat griddle over medium heat and lightly grease with vegetable oil. Using a 1/3 cup measuring cup, drop batter onto the hot griddle. When bubbles appear, flip and brown lightly on other side. Keep pancakes warm in oven until ready to serve.

   To serve, place 3 cakes on each plate. Top with 1 slice of salmon and a dollop of crème fraîche. Sprinkle with scallions or chives. Cakes are also delicious served with sliced grilled ham and maple syrup.

Serves 6

Crème Fraîche

6 oz. nonfat sour
   cream

2 T. finely chopped
   red onion

$\frac{1}{3}$ cup dry white wine

Blend all ingredients
and refrigerate.

Blueberry-Buttermilk Pancakes with Blueberry Butter

Innkeepers Jody Schmoll and Dennis Hayden
Blue Harbor House, Camden, ME

$\frac{3}{4}$ tsp. baking soda
1$\frac{1}{2}$ cups buttermilk
1$\frac{1}{2}$ cups all-purpose flour
$\frac{3}{4}$ cup whole wheat flour
$\frac{3}{4}$ cup large-flake rolled oats (optional)
$\frac{3}{4}$ tsp. baking powder
1 tsp. salt (optional)
1$\frac{1}{2}$ tsp. sugar
6 eggs, separated
4$\frac{1}{2}$ T. butter, melted
1$\frac{1}{2}$ cups milk
$\frac{1}{2}$ cup blueberries
Blueberry Butter (see recipe)

Dissolve baking soda in buttermilk. Sift flours, oats, baking powder, salt, and sugar together. Discard 1/4 of the egg yolks. Beat remaining yolks with melted butter. Mix into dry ingredients. Add buttermilk and milk, stirring to blend. In a separate bowl, beat egg whites until they stand in soft peaks; fold into batter.

Heat griddle over medium heat. Drop batter by spoonfuls onto hot griddle. Add a few blueberries to each pancake. Flip pancakes when evenly browned. Smother blueberry butter over pancakes and garnish with a few berries.

Serves 8

Blueberry Butter

$\frac{1}{2}$ cup butter, softened
$\frac{1}{3}$ cup confectioners' sugar
1 tsp. vanilla extract
10 oz. blueberries
$\frac{1}{4}$ cup shredded unsweetened coconut

In a food processor, mix butter, sugar, and vanilla into a thick paste. Add berries (saving a few for garnish) and coconut.

Orange Waffles

Innkeepers Diane and Hank Tremblay
Manor House, Norfolk, CT

2 cups all-purpose flour
3 tsp. baking powder
2 T. sugar
$\frac{1}{2}$ tsp. salt
4 eggs, lightly beaten
1 cup milk
4 T. butter, melted
3 T. grated orange zest

Preheat waffle iron. Sift together flour, baking powder, sugar, and salt. In a separate bowl, combine eggs, milk, and butter. Add orange zest. Add dry ingredients to wet ingredients in two equal parts, beating well after each addition until batter is smooth. Pour about 3/4 to 1 cup of batter at a time onto waffle iron. Bake until waffles are golden brown.

Yields 8 waffles

"Seems like a man could have something else for breakfast besides eggs."

— John Wayne in "Tycoon"

About Rockwell House Inn

Most Known For:
great hospitality and delicious breakfasts

Years in Business:
8

Most Popular Table:
"Courting Corner"

Chef: Debra Krohn

Education/Training:
Self-taught chef and baker

Influences:
healthful cooking

Hobbies:
triathlons, rug hooking

Favorite Foods:
fresh fruit, anything spicy

Sticky French Toast

Chef/Owner/Innkeeper Debra Krohn
Rockwell House Inn, Bristol, RI

1 stick ($\frac{1}{4}$ lb.) butter
1 cup brown sugar
2 T. corn syrup
1 large loaf French bread, cut into 16 ($\frac{3}{4}$") slices
8 eggs, beaten
2 cups milk
1 T. vanilla

In small saucepan, bring butter, brown sugar, and corn syrup to a simmer. Remove from heat and pour into 9x12" baking dish. Place bread on top of syrup. Mix eggs with milk and vanilla. Pour over bread. Cover and refrigerate over-night. Preheat oven to 350°. Uncover and bake for 30 minutes. Serve each person 2 slices.

Serves 8

Dutch Apple French Toast

Owner Lorie Whissell
Angel of the Sea, Cape May, NJ

$\frac{3}{4}$ cup butter
3 T. dark corn syrup
$1\frac{1}{2}$ cups brown sugar
4 apples, peeled, cored, and sliced
1 loaf cinnamon raisin bread, sliced, crusts removed
8 eggs
1 quart milk
$1\frac{1}{2}$ tsp. vanilla

Heat butter, corn syrup, and sugar until syrupy. Pour into a 10x15" pan. Spread apples over syrup. Layer bread slices over apples. Beat remaining ingredients together and pour the mixture over the bread. Refrigerate overnight. Bake in preheated 350° oven for 45 minutes.

Serves 10 to 12

Apple Stuffed French Toast with Crème Anglaise

Head Chef Wayne Cousins
Norumbega Inn, Camden, ME

4 Granny Smith apples, peeled, cored, and sliced
$\frac{1}{2}$ tsp. lemon juice
$\frac{1}{4}$ cup water
$\frac{1}{4}$ cup sugar
1 tsp. allspice
1 T. plus 1 tsp. cinnamon
2 tsp. nutmeg
12 slices sourdough bread
4 eggs
$\frac{1}{4}$ cup heavy cream
1 tsp. vanilla extract
oil to coat pan
Crème Anglaise (see recipe)

In sauté pan, place apples, lemon juice, water, sugar, allspice, 1 tablespoon cinnamon, and 1 teaspoon nutmeg. Cook slowly over medium heat, stirring occasionally, until apples are soft. Remove mixture from heat and cool.

In a bowl, whip together eggs, cream, vanilla, 1 teaspoon cinnamon, and 1 teaspoon nutmeg.

Place a layer of apples between 2 pieces of bread. Continue with remaining apples and bread. Heat oil in skillet over medium heat. Dip "sandwiches" into egg mixture, coating evenly. Cook on one side until brown; turn and brown on other side. Top with crème anglaise.

Serves 6

Crème Anglaise

$\frac{1}{2}$ cup sugar
1 pt. heavy cream
1 T. vanilla extract
3 egg yolks

Heat sugar, cream, and vanilla to just under boiling point. Add a little of the hot cream mix to egg yolks. Whisk rapidly; then add back to cream, whisking frequently until mixture thickens.

Wild Maine Blueberry Streusel French Toast

Owner/Innkeeper Kim O'Mahoney
The Inn at Portsmouth Harbor, Kittery, ME

Blueberry Syrup

1 cup Cran-Grape juice
2 T. cornstarch
4 cups blueberries (The tiny wild ones from Maine are the best!)
$\frac{3}{4}$ to 1 cup sugar
juice of 1 lemon

In a saucepan, whisk together juice and cornstarch. Add berries, sugar, and lemon juice. Bring to a boil over medium heat, stirring constantly. Boil about 5 minutes until thickened.

1 loaf raisin bread
6 extra large eggs
$1\frac{1}{2}$ cups milk (Nonfat works fine.)
1 cup whipping cream (Nonfat half-and-half works too!)
2 tsp. pure vanilla extract
1 tsp. cinnamon
$\frac{1}{2}$ tsp. freshly grated nutmeg
$\frac{1}{4}$ cup butter
$\frac{1}{2}$ cup brown sugar
$\frac{1}{2}$ cup chopped walnuts or pecans
Blueberry Syrup (see recipe)

The night before, coat 7x11" baking dish with nonstick spray. Layer bread slices in overlapping rows. Whisk together eggs, milk, vanilla, cinnamon, and nutmeg; pour slowly over bread. Cover with plastic wrap and press down to submerge bread. Refrigerate overnight.

In the morning, preheat oven to 350°. Melt butter in saucepan. Add brown sugar and nuts and combine. Remove plastic wrap from bread and top with melted butter mixture. Bake 40 minutes.

Remove from oven. Let stand 5 to 10 minutes before serving with blueberry syrup.

Serves 6

Cranberry Orange Muffins

Head Chef Wayne Cousins
Norumbega Inn, Camden, ME

2 cups cake flour or $1\frac{3}{4}$ cups all-purpose flour
$\frac{3}{4}$ tsp. salt
$\frac{1}{4}$ cup sugar
2 tsp. double-acting baking powder
2 eggs, beaten
2 to 4 T. melted butter
$\frac{1}{2}$ cup milk
$\frac{1}{4}$ cup orange juice concentrate, thawed
1 cup cranberries
1 T. orange zest

Preheat oven to 350°. Grease and flour 12 muffin cups. Combine first 4 ingredients in a large bowl. In separate bowl, mix eggs, butter, milk, and orange juice. Combine both mixtures. Fold in cranberries and orange zest. Pour batter into prepared muffin cups. Bake 10 to 15 minutes.

Yields 1 dozen muffins

About Norumbega Inn

Most Known For:
luxurious accomodations and gourmet food

Years in Business:
12

Chef:
Wayne Cousins

Education/Training:
on hands training; father is a culinary teacher

Influences:
"It's in my blood. I come from a line of chefs."

Hobbies:
writing new recipes

Hometown:
Beleas, ME

Favorite Foods:
seafood

Favorite Cookbooks:
Gourmet magazine

Verry Berry Streusel Muffins

Innkeeper/Owner Sue H. Carroll
Mainstay Inn, Cape May, NJ

2 cups all-purpose flour
$\frac{1}{2}$ cup sugar
2 tsp. baking powder
$\frac{1}{2}$ tsp. baking soda
$\frac{1}{2}$ tsp. salt
1 (8 oz.) container lemon yogurt
$\frac{1}{2}$ cup vegetable oil
1 tsp. grated lemon zest
2 eggs
$\frac{1}{2}$ cup fresh raspberries
$\frac{1}{2}$ cup fresh blueberries
Streusel Topping (see recipe)

Preheat oven to 400°. Grease 12 muffin cups.

In a large bowl, combine flour, sugar, baking powder, baking soda, and salt. Mix well. In a small bowl, combine yogurt, oil, lemon zest, and eggs. Mix well. Add to the flour mixture, stirring just until the dry ingredients are moistened. Gently stir in raspberries and blueberries. Fill the prepared muffin cups.

Sprinkle topping over the batter and bake for 18 to 20 minutes or until a wooden toothpick inserted in center comes out clean. Cool muffins on wire rack. Serve warm or at room temperature.

Yields 12 muffins

Streusel Topping

$\frac{1}{3}$ cup sugar
$\frac{1}{4}$ cup all-purpose flour
2 T. butter

In a small bowl, combine sugar and flour. Using a pastry blender or 2 knives, cut in butter until the mixture is crumbly.

Shiitake-Cheddar Cheese Muffins

Executive Chef Carl V. Colucci
Le Palais, Resorts Casino, Atlantic City

4 oz. shiitake mushrooms, stems removed
4 T. butter
2 cups all-purpose flour
$2\frac{1}{2}$ tsp. baking powder
$\frac{1}{2}$ tsp. salt
$1\frac{1}{2}$ T. sugar
3 T. Dijon mustard
1 cup shredded Cheddar cheese
1 cup milk
2 eggs

Preheat oven to 375°. Grease muffin tins generously.

Sauté mushrooms in butter until tender. Cool and reserve. In a mixing bowl, combine flour, baking powder, salt, and sugar. In a separate bowl, combine remaining ingredients and mushrooms. Incorporate into flour mixture; combine well. Spoon batter into the prepared muffins tins, filling them 3/4 full. Bake 20 minutes or until toothpick inserted into muffin comes out dry.

Yields approximately 12 muffins

Spicy Pumpkin Bread

Innkeeper Marie Brophy
Isaiah Hall B&B Inn, Dennis (Cape Cod), MA

1 cup brown sugar, firmly packed
$\frac{1}{3}$ cup vegetable shortening
2 eggs
1 cup canned pumpkin
$\frac{1}{4}$ cup milk
2 cups all-purpose flour
2 tsp. baking powder
$\frac{1}{4}$ tsp. baking soda
$\frac{1}{2}$ tsp. salt
1 tsp. ground cloves
$\frac{1}{2}$ cup chopped walnuts and/or $\frac{1}{2}$ cup raisins

Preheat oven to 350°. Cream together sugar and shortening. Beat in eggs. Add pumpkin and milk; mix together well.

In a separate bowl, stir together flour, baking powder, baking soda, salt, and cloves. Add this to wet ingredients. Stir in walnuts and/or raisins. Pour into a greased 9x5" loaf pan. Bake 55 to 60 minutes. Cool 10 minutes. Remove from pan and cool on rack.

Yields 10 slices

Sweet Potato Cranberry Bread

Innkeeper Virginia S. Donnelly
Candleberry Inn on Cape Cod, Brewster, MA

3 large eggs
1$\frac{1}{2}$ cups sugar
1$\frac{1}{2}$ cups mashed sweet potatoes
1 cup vegetable oil
2 tsp. vanilla extract
2$\frac{1}{4}$ cups all-purpose flour
1 tsp. salt
1$\frac{1}{2}$ tsp. EACH baking powder, baking soda, and cinnamon
$\frac{1}{2}$ tsp. EACH ground cloves, ginger, and nutmeg
1 cup dried cranberries

Preheat oven to 350°. Grease and flour two 8" loaf pans.
   In a large mixing bowl, combine eggs, sugar, sweet potatoes, oil, and vanilla and mix. In a separate bowl, combine dry ingredients and spices; add to sweet potato mixture and mix only to blend. Fold in cranberries. Pour batter into loaf pans. Bake 50 to 60 minutes.

Yields 20 slices

"I'm a bagel on a plate full of onion rolls."

—Barbra Streisand in "Funny Girl"

Particating Restaurants,

Maine

124 Cottage Street Restaurant, Bar Harbor
Rose Garden Restaurant at Bar Harbor Hotel, Bar Harbor
Blue Harbor House, Camden
Gypsy Sweethearts Restaurant, Ogunquit
The Inn at Portsmouth Harbor, Kittery
Norumbega Inn, Camden

New Hampshire

Acorns Restaurant, Durham
The Dolphin Striker Restaurant, Portsmouth
The Friendly Toast, Portsmouth
La Bec Rouge, Hampton
Three Chimneys Inn, Durham

Massachusetts

Candleberry Inn on Cape Cod, Brewster
Christian's Restaurant, Chatham
Coonamessett Inn, Falmouth
Isaiah Hall B&B Inn, Dennis
The Marlborough House, Woods Hole
Martin House Restaurant, Provincetown
Mews Restaurant, Provincetown
The Old Manse Inn & Restaurant, Brewster
The Paddock Restaurant, Hyannis
Vorelli's Restaurant, Provincetown
Wequassett Inn, Chatham
The Woodbox Inn, Nantucket

Rhode Island

The Beech Tree Inn, Newport
The Mooring Restaurant, Newport
Rockwell House Inn, Bristol

Hotels, and Inns

Connecticut

Centro Ristorante & Bar, Darien
Manor House, Norfolk
Red Brook Inn, Old Mystic

New York

1880 House, Westhampton
Gurney's Inn, Montauk
Southampton Publick House, Southampton

New Jersey

Alexander's Inn, Cape May
Angel of the Sea, Cape May
Bally's Park Place, Atlantic City
Bridges Restaurant on the Bay, Ocean City
The Chalfonte Hotel, Cape May
C'est La Vie Restaurant, Beach Haven Crest
Doris & Ed's, Highlands
East Bay Crab and Grille, Egg Harbor Township
The Ebbit Room, Cape May
Fredric's Restaurant, West Creek
Green Cuisine Restaurant, Stone Harbor
Green Gables Restaurant and Inn, Beach Haven
Henry's on the Beach, Cape May

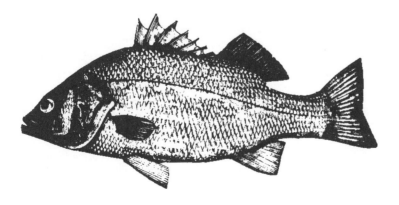

More Restaurants, Hotels, and Inns

New Jersey (cont.)

Il Pescature, Ocean City
The Inn at Sugar Hill, Mays Landing
Le Palais, Resorts Casino, Atlantic City
The Mad Batter Restaurant at the Carroll Villa Hotel, Cape May
Mainstay Inn, Cape May
Mama Mia's Ristorante, Seaville
Peaches at Sunset, Cape May
The Queen Victoria, Cape May
Ram's Head Inn, Absecon
Redingtons Fine Seafood Restaurant, Point Pleasant
The Tun Tavern Brewey & Restaurant, Atlantic City
Van Scoy's Bistro, Cape May
Waters Edge Restaurant, Cape May

Delaware

Barry's Gull Cottage B&B, Dewey Beach
Boathouse Restaurant, Bethany Beach
Celsius Restaurant and Tapas, Rehoboth Beach
Harry's Savoy Grille, Wilmington
Nantuckets, Fenwick Isle
The Terrace at Greenhill, Wilmington
Woody's Restaurant, Rehoboth Beach

Maryland

Galaxy Bar & Grille, Ocean City
Phillips by the Sea, Ocean City

Index

About the Author

Name:
Connie Correia Fisher

Education/Training:
Johnson & Wales
University

Influences:
the seasons,
cravings

Hobbies:
movies, reading,
trash picking, writing,
restoring furniture

Hometown:
Cherry Hill, NJ

Favorite Foods:
panzanella with
Jersey tomatoes,
pasta, Bill's choco-
late chip cookies,
seafood

Favorite Cookbook:
*Local Flavor, The
Rittenhouse
Cookbook, White
Dog Cafe Cookbook*

Maine

Tourism Association
207-623-0363

Bureau of Parks and Lands
207-287-3821

Islands available for recreation
207-287-3821

New Hampshire

Office of Travel & Tourism Development
603-271-2343 or 800-386-4664

Division of Parks and Recreation
603-271-3556

Massachusetts

Office of Travel and Tourism
617-727-3201 or 800-447-6277

Bureau of Recreation
617-727-3180

Division of Fisheries and Wildlife
617-727-3151

Rhode Island

Tourism Division
401-277-2601 or 800-556-2484

Department of Environmental Management
401-277-3075

Division of Environmental Management
401-647-3367 or 800-280-2267

Connecticut

Department of Economic Development
800-282-6863

Department of Environmental Protection
860-424-3200

Travel Information

New York

Division of Tourism
800-225-5697

Convention and Visitors Bureau
212-397-8222

Office of Parks, Recreation, and Historic Preservation
518-474-0456

Division of Fish and Wildlife
518-457-3521

New Jersey

Division of Travel and Tourism
609-633-2623

Division of Parks and Forestry
609-292-2733

Historic Preservation Office
609-984-0176

State Forestry Services
609-292-2520

State Park Service
609-292-2772

Delaware

Tourism Office
302-739-4271 or 800-441-8846

Division of Parks and Recreation
302-739-4702

Divison of Fish and Wildlife
302-739-4431

Maryland

Office of Tourism Development
800-394-5725

Department of Natural Resources
410-260-8186

Department of Natural Resources
800-688-3467

About the Editor

Name:
Joanne Correia

Education/Training:
Temple University

Influences:
the numerous recipes seen since working with my daughter

Hobbies:
stitchery, bike riding, church choir, spending time with family — especially Matthew

Hometown:
Cherry Hill, NJ

Favorite Foods:
quick breads, pasta, sautéed vegetables

Favorite Cookbook:
Betty Crocker's New Picture Cook Book, Local Flavor

Notes

Notes

Notes

Notes

Small Potatoes Press Order Form

Please send the following:

☐ ____ copies of ***Coastal Cuisine: Seaside Recipes from Maine to Maryland***
    - $11.95

☐ ____ copies of ***PB&J USA*** - $10.95

☐ ____ copies of ***Local Flavor: Favorite Recipes of Philadelphia Area*** - $15.95

Sales Tax: ***Coastal Cuisine:*** NJ addresses please add $.96 (6%)

              PB&J USA: NJ addresses please add $.72 (6%)

              Local Flavor: NJ addresses please add $.96 (6%)

Shipping: $3.00 for the first book; $1.50 for each additional book

Payment: Please make your check or money order payable to:

Small Potatoes Press
1106 Stokes Avenue, Collingswood, NJ 08108
609-869-5207

SHIP TO: _____

_____

☐ Is this a gift? If so, please include your name, full address, phone number, and any message you'd like to have autographed on the book.

_____

_____

_____

_____

Thank you!